CROSSING'S
DARTMOOR
WORKER

CROSSING'S
DARTMOOR
WORKER

A facsimile of the first edition,
edited and introduced by
Brian Le Messurier

With a new introduction by Crispin Gill

**Peninsula
Press**

ACKNOWLEDGEMENTS

are made for the following photographs

The Author, opposite p. 10, Mr J. Collins; *The Farmer*, opposite p. 11, Lady Sayer; *The Farmer*, opposite p. 26, Lady Sayer; *The Labourer*, opposite p. 27, Lady Sayer; *The Newtake Wall Builder*, opposite p. 27, from Vol 4 of *Dartmoor Pictorial Records*; *Swaling*, opposite p. 42, Mr J. Endacott; *Peat Cutting*, opposite p. 42, Messrs Chapman & Son; *Peat Cutting*, opposite p. 43, top, Messrs Chapman & Son; *Peat Cutting* opposite p. 43, bottom, Mr. J. Endacott; *The Warrener*, opposite p. 58, top, Methuen & Co Ltd; *The Warrener*, opposite p. 58, bottom, Mrs E. M. Vanstone; *The Miner*, opposite p. 59, top, Lady Sayer; *The Miner*, opposite p. 59, bottom, Mr G. W. A. Shepherd; *The Clay Labourer*, opposite p. 74; top and bottom, Lady Sayer; *The Sportsman*, opposite p. 75, Lady Sayer; *The Sportsman*, opposite p. 90, Lady Sayer; *Under Canvas*, opposite p. 91, Plymouth Central Library; *The Antiquary*, opposite p. 106, top, from Vol 4 of *Dartmoor Pictorial Records*; *The Antiquary*, opposite p. 106, bottom, Lady Sayer; *Coaching*, opposite p. 107, Mrs G. Moir; *The Artist*, opposite p. 107, Lydford House Hotel; *'In along' and 'Out auver'*, opposite p. 122, top, Valentine & Sons Ltd; *'In along' and 'Out auver'*, opposite p. 122, bottom, Mr A. Stevens; *The Hotelier*, opposite p. 123, Mr. A. Stevens.

Published by Peninsula Press Ltd
P.O. Box 31
Newton Abbot
Devon TQ12 5XH

Tel 0803 875875

Printed in Great Britain by
Redwood Press, Melksham, Wiltshire

Cased edition ISBN 1 872640 19 2
Paperback ISBN 1 872640 20 6

CONTENTS

INTRODUCTION TO THE 1992 EDITION

Crispin Gill

To say that Dartmoor has changed in the hundred years since William Crossing wrote this book, the *Dartmoor Worker*, is to state the obvious, for all the world has changed. The Moor may not have altered much to the eye: Crossing would still be more at home there today than a city dweller would be in his city. The real change is in the people. If one works through Crossing's chapter heads, it soon becomes apparent.

The farmer is still there, of course, but in far fewer numbers. Some of the old names survive, like Coaker of Runnage. But many of the smaller farmhouses are now ruins, in some cases barely detectable from the earlier buildings of the tin miners. Others have become adventure training centres. Farmers can still be seen tending their cattle and their sheep on horseback, but young lads out on those go-anywhere motor cycles are not unknown herding cattle.

Even in Crossing's day, the moorman was not what he had been earlier. The labourer has largely vanished. On the roads the parish lengthman is replaced by gangs of labourers, highly mechanised. Where the county council needs to build a new wall, or repair an old one where it flanks a county road, there are men who can apply the ancient skills. Newtake walls proper are no longer built, but where a landowner or farmer can find some claim to the ownership of a stretch of moorland he encloses it with a wire fence. Some of these stretch for miles, and bar access far more effectively than the old walls. Inside these fences too the farmer often clears the ground with mechanical cutters and uses fertilisers to improve the grazing. In so doing he changes the nature of the vegetation.

A long campaign against indiscriminate burning of heather has reduced the amount of vandalism that Crossing complained of. What is done seems to be better controlled, but with fewer men working on fewer farms there is doubt as to whether as much is done today. Large flocks of sheep and herds of cattle still graze the Moor along with the ponies, very often put there to gain the subsidies that were not available in Crossing's day.

Peat was still being cut extensively as a domestic fuel right up to 1914, but even Crossing notes that its use was falling off. Now commercial cutting has disappeared altogether. The warrener, the man who tended the artificial rabbit burrows, has vanished as well. The warren houses are like farmhouses given over to parties of youngsters, and the rabbits have yielded place to the industrial archaeologist.

In 1903 there were still mines being worked on the Moor, and I have known old men living on the moor fringes who worked during the week at mines deep into the Moor. One who lived in a cottage at the bottom of Shadycoombe, Hooe Meavy, had been a tool sharpener at a mine the other side of Fox Tor Mires. He would walk out on the Monday morning with his food for the week, and come home at the end of the week for a bath, a change of clothes and another week's supply. Now not a single mine is operating on Dartmoor. Rows of former miners' cottages stand empty, the leats that carried their water for motive power are mainly dry, and in-country men no longer make the long weekly trek out.

Just one quarry, at Merrivale, now works on the Moor proper, and the rest are abandoned. Cottages stand empty. China clay is still dug with its pits getting deeper and the spoil heaps higher. The pits that continue, however, are very much on the fringe and, apart from Lee Moor and Wotter, the workers live off the Moor altogether.

Whortleberries still flourish on the Moor but no one goes 'out-over' to pick them now commercially. Indeed I doubt if many people pick them at all, but are content to buy blueberries from their supermarkets. Not that they are ever so good.

Hunting attracts even more followers than ever, and the packs are as strong. There are more anglers, certainly in the reservoirs that a century ago were fewer in number and even those were new invasions. The huge summer camps of the Volunteers—in 1884 there were 3,500 men under canvas at Hey Tor—are all gone; the Territorials and regular soldiers who use the Moor are housed at Okehampton or Willsworthy in more permanent accomodation in much smaller numbers.

Prison officers still make up the population of Princetown, though they do not supervise working parties from horseback, nor carry carbines over their shoulder. The antiquary is with us in greater numbers than ever, though he calls himself an archaeologist nowadays and is liable to be as excited over a vermin trap or a mining survival as a stone row. These industrial archaeologists are a new breed altogether. Artists come and go, and the purple hills of the Widgerys crop up with less skill and more facility as tourist bait in the moor edge towns and villages. To the painters we now have to add potters.

In Crossing's time the visitor was a middle class character who stayed in a hotel on or near the Moor. Rather scornfully he suggests that they never walked even a mile or two away from their base. If they went exploring they would take one of the coaches that plied up and down the main roads of the Moor, and so saw little that was not visible from the vehicle.

The same could be said today of the hordes who flock to Dartmoor by car. In summer the road out from Torquay is nearly solid with the cars of the holiday-maker, and places like Widecombe almost impossible to get into. Were Crossing writing now about the occupations of Dartmoor he would devote a chapter to the keepers of gift shops and tearooms. A major recreation now of the car owner—which means nearly everybody—is the Sunday or fine evening run out in the car, with a call at a 'country pub' for a drink or a meal.

As a result roads have had to be widened and pubs have changed out of recognition. They are more restaurants, more geared for the urban visitor with their carpets and brassware and plush furniture, than places where the local can have a quiet pint of an evening. It is a revolution that has been wrought entirely by the motor car.

But on the Moor itself there are probably as many people now, if not more, than there were working in Crossing's time. There are far more people walking seriously, and with knowledge of where they are going and what they are seeing. Even in the remotest parts now, where one has stopped to drink in the seemingly infinite space and silence of Dartmoor, a few walkers, booted, cagouled and well-mapped, will come up over the skyline. It is not as bad as Snowdonia, where climbers queue beneath the popular routes. Probably far more people have a deeper knowledge of the Moor, its history and its lonely places, more understand its solitude, its solace and its beauty, than ever before.

William Crossing wrote this book as a series of newspaper articles when he was over fifty. A lifetime of walking the Moor in all weathers (and without the protective clothing that we enjoy today, or the motor car to carry him close to his objective) had limited his explorations with gout and rheumatism. In many ways he was writing about the closing decades of the last century. So this book is invaluable to us, as a record of the way life has changed.

But although it has changed—peat ties have fallen in, the mechanical mining aids of the last century are as hard to find as the blowing houses of earlier times, the TV mast on North Hessary nods over so many skylines, the shiny tin boxes of modern cars seem everywhere—the essential Dartmoor has not changed.

Its peace, its austere beauty, its loneliness, its feeling of wilderness, of essential values is still there. Crossing more than most men has made it accessible, and understandable, to us.

Crispin Gill
February 1992

INTRODUCTION TO THE 1966 EDITION

Brian Le Messurier

THE subject matter of this book first appeared in *The Western Morning News* as a series of articles by William Crossing under the general title 'Present-day life on Dartmoor' in 1903. The topics dealt with were not used elsewhere. In 'Present-day life . . .' he was concerned with the ordinary people of the moor and with visitors to it. In his books he concentrated on the scenery, the prehistoric remains, folklore, and history. Crossing at first contracted to write nineteen articles but added the last to complete the round score. They were published on Wednesdays beginning on 5 August 1903.

The passing of sixty-three years has given the articles an historical value. Dartmoor life has undergone great changes and some of the old occupations have gone forever. With the designation of Devon as a rabbit clearance area in 1956 it became legally impossible to follow the warrener's trade, and peat cutting is practically forgotten—at least in the way Crossing described it. Nowhere else can one find such detailed descriptions of life on the moor at the beginning of the century. Crossing takes the reader over the horse-drawn coach excursion routes; he bids us accompany the warrener as he sets his nets in the chill of a Dartmoor night; we join the moorman riding across southern Dartmoor searching for a lost bullock and look over the artist's shoulder as he sketches the landscape.

He has some shrewd comments to make concerning visitors to the moor, and in the chapter 'The Guide' he expounds his ideas for the perfect Dartmoor guide-book. It is interesting to see that in 1903 he had already worked out the plan on which he was to write his *Guide to Dartmoor*.[1] When the 'Present-day life . . .' series ended *The Western Morning News* printed a paragraph

[1] Republished 1990 by Peninsula Press

which read : 'Mr Crossing has much to say on the imperfections of the ordinary guide-books to Dartmoor. No man, assuredly, is better qualified to give an opinion as to such productions, for Mr Crossing has, admittedly, no superior, if any equal, in his knowledge of the forest under all conditions of wind and weather. The thought naturally arises in the mind of the readers of this paper; why should not Mr Crossing himself write the ideal Dartmoor guide-book?' Even earlier, in 'A Hundred Years on Dartmoor', he had had some strong things to say on the subject, but here, for the first time, he revealed the method he was to use with such success in 1909. Crossing, however, was waiting for more congenial circumstances before setting down what was already in his head and jotted down in thirty years of note-taking.

A summary of Crossing's life was included in the introduction to the 1965 edition of the *Guide* so there is no need for repetition here, but it should be mentioned that for many years Crossing earned his living solely from his West Country writings. Various editorial commissions had come his way in the nineties and he had published a few books, but with the end of the century, at the age of fifty-three, he turned to the newspapers to provide him with a regular income. By now he had begun to feel the effects of the gout and rheumatism which were to tax him so severely in later life, and it was easier for him to stay at home writing regular weekly articles worked up from his notes than contributing to what he must have regarded as tiresome pot-boilers : such publications as the *Mount Edgecumbe Souvenir* (1899) and *The Book of Fair Devon* (1900). *The Marine and River Guide to the South Coast of Devon and Cornwall* also came out about this time and required a good deal of research 'on the ground'.

'A Hundred Years on Dartmoor' (*The Western Morning News*, 1900) was the first newspaper series, and was followed by 'The Teign from Moor to Sea' (*Mid-Devon & Newton Times*, 1900), 'Echoes of an Ancient Forest' (*The Western Morning News*, 1901), 'Gems in a Granite Setting' (*The Western Morning News*, 1902), 'Folk Rhymes of Devon' (*Devon Evening Express*, 1902),

'Westcountry People and Places' (*Western Weekly News*, 1902), 'Present-day life on Dartmoor' (*The Western Morning News*, 1903) and 'The Stones of Dartmoor and their story' (*The Western Morning News*, 1904). 'A Hundred Years . . .' 'Gems . . .' and 'Folk Rhymes . . .' were later published as books, the last-named not until 1911, and then greatly revised. 'Westcountry People and Places' went on with some breaks until 1909.

As one reads Crossing's words in the book that follows it is hard to understand the difficulties with which he had to contend. When a young man he had broken his right arm and it had never set properly. This malformation was not helped by his worsening rheumatic condition, and his writing became jerky and laboured. He and his wife lived in a small cottage at Brent Tor until they moved to Mary Tavy in the summer of 1902; from here Crossing was able to make occasional visits to the moor and kept up to date with Dartmoor events. He was always short of money. Towards the end of 1904 the intelligentsia came to the rescue.

TESTIMONIAL TO MR WILLIAM CROSSING

Some time since a suggestion was made that Mr William Crossing, the well-known writer on Dartmoor subjects, was deserving of some recognition, as having done much to popularise the moorlands and spread a knowledge of their beauties. The present seems to be a fitting opportunity to show appreciation of the value of his work; and it is thought that the presentation of a purse would best accomplish this and be most acceptable to him. For some time past he has been afflicted with illness, and his pen, upon which he is entirely dependent, has been partly laid aside.

We are familiar with the circumstances, and consider that a helping hand is absolutely necessary and deserved; and we appeal with confidence to all who have enjoyed and profited by the books and articles written by Mr Crossing on Dartmoor, to aid in this.

Contributions sent to Mr A Rowe, the Duchy Hotel, Prince-town, will be thankfully received and acknowledged.

(signed) CLIFFORD   A. T. QUILLER-COUCH
         ROBERT BURNARD   ARTH. W. JEFFERY
         S. BARING-GOULD   AARON ROWE
         EDEN PHILLPOTTS   ERNEST CROFT
                             J. BROOKING ROWE

This was, quite simply, an appeal for funds, but it was poorly supported. A lady wrote to *The Western Morning News* in the following February: 'The wretchedly inadequate nature of the response is a serious reflection upon the judgment and generosity of all Westerners. . . .'

It is against this background of illness and near-poverty, there-fore, that we should read this book, and anything else Crossing wrote during this trying period of his life. But the reader will find no trace of bitterness or self-pity in the lines that follow; instead an impish sense of humour shines through.[1]

Few changes have been made to the articles as originally printed, and Crossing's prose style is unaltered. No attempt has been made to introduce the modern form of place-name spelling, but these have been standardised within the book and the index added. The photographs have all been specially chosen. It is hoped that collectively they add a visual dimension to the author's wonderful word pictures. Acknowledgments are given opposite the contents page, but I must particularly thank Lady Sayer for giving me *carte blanche* to use any photographs I cared to select from the unique collection of her grandfather, Robert Burnard.

BRIAN LE MESSURIER
February 1966

[1] Crossing held out, and in 1906 his fortunes changed, for he became tutor to the sons of Mr W. P. Collins. With a steady income he was able to concentrate on his *Guide to Dartmoor*.

Appendix to the 1966 Introduction

I am glad to have the opportunity, twenty-six years after the book's original appearance, to add a few words to my original Introduction.

Crossing's Dartmoor Worker—the title was conferred by David St John Thomas of the publishers, David & Charles—is eagerly read by a public for whom social history and industrial archaeology have become vogue subjects. The book has been out of print for many years, and second-hand copies were much sought after.

The original Introduction is retained as written, and I would change nothing I wrote in 1966. I have had to amend little in the text. However, I should say that an elderly Bovey Tracey lady, Miss Olive Bent, did tell me in 1969 that William Crossing was wrong to state (page 107) that Mr Hodge was chief warder. He was chief mason instructor.

The book now contains an additional photograph, of William Widgery the artist, and I am grateful to Mr Ron Boulter of the Lydford House Hotel which was built by Widgery, for letting me use it. A few of the other picture captions have been brought up to date, or additional information given.

I also thank Lady Sayer for once again giving her gracious consent for the book to be illustrated with many photographs from the collection of her grandfather, Robert Burnard.

Brian Le Messurier
February 1992

The Author   William Crossing, shortly before he died in 1928

The Farmer Teign Head farm: probably the oldest picture of it extant. The farm is now totally ruinous. Photograph by Robert Burnard, 12 August 1889

THE FARMER

THOUGH the chief attractions of Dartmoor are undoubtedly its scenery, its antiquities and historical associations, it is also acknowledged that its modern side is by no means deficient in interest. That the former, however, impart to the latter much of this is certain. The old and the new live side by side on the moor, and it is almost impossible to look upon that which is of today without seeing how it is affected by that which is ancient. While pursuits similar to those of the rural lowlands exist there, they yet present features of their own. The soil and climate, the scarcity of roads, and the absence of trees, of course contribute in a great measure to this, but they are not the sole causes of it. The influence of an older day is still felt; there is a link with the past that has not been broken. Instead of hedges the fields are enclosed with rough stone walls; shelter such as the in-country farmer enjoys is unknown to his brother on the moor. The labourer has often to walk a long distance to his work, perhaps through a wild and solitary district, and to cross streams and bogs. The aspect of things is altogether different from those beyond the verge of the moor; the conditions are not the same. Plantations, roads, railways, and the growth of villages have done much to alter that which the lowland husbandman looks upon; the Dartmoor farmer sees the face of the country almost as it was centuries ago. And it is for the reason that he does so, because his work lies amid so much that is unchanged, that it possesses a special interest for us.

Less than a century ago Dartmoor was comparatively little known, and was regarded as an almost inaccessible region. Those who wrote of it describe it as a rocky desert, subject to furious storms. Carrington speaks of it as a land 'untrod,' and of its 'half-savage peasant,' and though he must be allowed a poet's licence

11

there is not much doubt that his descriptions in the main reflected the ideas regarding it which were entertained in his time.
A French writer, Jules Poulain, who it is evident had some
acquaintance with the district, calls the moor 'une terre inconnu,'
and makes one of his characters doubt its existence. Many similar
instances might be cited to prove that the majority of those to
whom Dartmoor was known only by name looked upon it as
meriting the description of M. Catel, when he called it 'un vraie
Siberie.'

But the book that was sealed to our grandsires lies open before
us; the moor is no longer an unknown land. It may not prove
uninteresting if we look into its pages, for it has much to reveal.
We may read something of the people who have made that wild
region their home, and of the influences which mould their lives.
The agriculturist, the herdsman, the labourer, and others who
live upon the great moor, as well as those who seek it for
pleasure or profit, or who find there a field for antiquarian research, or discover subjects for the brush, may well claim our
notice. A picture of Dartmoor in the remote past can be constructed from the remains of the rude dwellings and the sepulchral
monuments that are scattered over its surface, but by the dim
light an examination of these affords it will be only an indistinct
one. The flickering beams of the torch held up before it enable
us to obtain no more than glimpses, yet even these charm by
leading us back into a world half real and half imaginative.
Upon the picture of the moor as it is today a clear light is thrown,
and yet it does not altogether lack the glamour of romance. We
can view it in its entirety; nothing is obscure, it is only strange.
Our knowledge of the race which dwelt upon the moor in days
long flown is but scant; our ideas concerning them formed in
great measure by wanderings in the realm of speculation. Of those
who at present inhabit it we can obtain a real acquaintance. Let
us then not seek to resuscitate the dead past, but turn our attention to the Dartmoor people of today, choosing for the purposes
of our remarks some typical examples of the classes to be found

there. The earliest occupation of man named in Holy Writ is that
of the tiller of the soil. It is the most important of his pursuits, and
since it is so the farmer may fittingly claim our first notice. We do
not propose to look upon his occupation from an economic stand-
point, but merely as it affects him as an individual.

The Dartmoor farms within the Forest are situated chiefly in
the valleys of the East and West Dart, and those of their tributaries
the Walla Brook and the Swincombe, and are most of them very
ancient. There is also a farm on the East Ockment, one on the
North, and another on the South Teign; fields belonging to
Huntingdon warren, on the Avon, and the large enclosures near
Princetown. Without the Forest there are farms on the branches
of the Mew, on the Walkham, and on the Tavy, while on every
stream they are seen running a short distance up into the moor.
But with two or three exceptions it is only through the Dart
valleys, and those branching from them, that the farmer has
penetrated far into the waste, and here his enclosures have been
formed for centuries, many of them probably being in existence
when the bounds of the Forest were first set out. While it is possible
that some of these farms grew out of the settlements of a much
earlier time, that is not the explanation of the existence of most of
them. It was certain advantages of soil and a comparatively
sheltered situation that caused the first Dartmoor farmers to settle
in this part of the moor.

Some of the Dartmoor farmhouses are lonely in the extreme.
Teign Head, approached only by a rough track, has no neighbour
nearer than Fernworthy, and that is at some distance from another
habitation. Except during the summer, when the rambler over
the moor may call in at the solitary house, or when the moorman
is abroad, there are no visitors at Teign Head. When the winter
season draws near the dwellers in that remote farm know that
ere the days will again grow long there will be periods, perhaps
of weeks, during which no stranger will enter the valley in which
it hides itself. One thing only will vary the monotony of their
existence—the appearance of the foxhounds or the harriers. Who,

again, but the huntsman is likely to visit Lough Tor Hole, on the
East Dart? Lost to view under a sheltering hill, and being near no
road, the farm is known to few but those living in the district. In
the bright summer days the wanderer might chance to stumble
upon it, but in the season when they are dull and drear the moor
does not know him, and Lough Tor Hole is then as though it were
a hundred miles from civilisation. Huntingdon, in the south
quarter of the Forest, is a mile and a half from the nearest house,
Hayford Hall, which itself is situated in a lonely spot on the
border of the common, and strangers are but seldom seen. Other
instances of houses standing in solitary places might be named,
none quite so remote as Teign Head, but yet far from the beaten
path. Indeed, unless it be in the little settlements on the moor,
such as Hexworthy and Pizwell, there are few Dartmoor farms
that are neighboured closely, and even there the houses are only
very few in number.

This isolation of his dwelling, and in the days when roads were
not as they are now it was much greater than at present, has had
its effect upon the Dartmoor farmer. Dependent almost entirely
upon his own efforts for everything that he needed, it made him
self-reliant, and this quality has been transmitted from father to
son. In cases where the in-country farmer would seek the aid of
the farrier or the smith, the Dartmoor man often performed their
work himself. Carpentry, rude it may have been, he was no
stranger to; even the box which, in place of a basket, he carried
with him to the river when he fished, and which was fashioned so
that it fitted against his side, was of his own manufacture. He
turned his hand to everything: having no one to help him he
helped himself. The impossibility of obtaining anything beyond
necessaries in the matter of food, and with no great choice of
those, caused him to give no thought to luxuries, and so he grew
up hardy, while a sufficiency on his table of such as his farm
yielded made him contented.

The last few years have altered much of this; there has been
a change in the conditions of the Dartmoor farmer's life, but it

has not deprived him of his sterling qualities. The district in which he dwells is still a wild one, and he occupies, if not in every case the house of his forefathers, one raised on its site, but he is more in touch with the outer world. The railway has reached the verge of the Forest, and the telegraph wire has been carried far into it. Still, he is so situated as to recognise the benefit of his early training, and has not been rendered less independent because he feels that it is in his power to get much done for him that his father would have had to do unaided. Advantages are within easier reach than formerly, it is true; but he is yet on Dartmoor, and Dartmoor, as he will tell you, is not a forty-acre field.

One peculiarity of the Dartmoor man is the friendliness with which he regards those among whom he dwells, though it is only what we should expect to find in a region possessing such natural characteristics as the moor. Each knows the difficulties consequent upon the climate and causes such as are not met with elsewhere, with which the other has to contend, and each strives to render aid to the other when it is needed. There is a bond of union between them, stronger than is found in the lowlands. A neighbourly feeling, of course, exists in the latter; in no parish would it be found that a farmer refused help to another when it was wanted, but on Dartmoor this is more marked, and is by no means confined to outdoor operations. The women are equally ready with the men to render assistance, and household duties are cheerfully undertaken by neighbours in cases of illness and such like. One reason for this community feeling is to be found in the fact that the majority of the moorland dwellers have grown up together. As children they learned the same tasks; as youths and maidens they were taught the same duties, performing them almost within sight of each other; and as men and women their choice of wives and husbands was made from among themselves. Each has always known nearly every one around him, and feels himself to belong to one brotherhood.

The weekly journey to the nearest market town is looked

forward to by the Dartmoor farmer or his wife, as it is by those who dwell in the in-country, and this, and an occasional day with the hounds during the season, forms his principal recreation. His hospitality to strangers is well known. The policy of the open door obtains on Dartmoor, but the visitor has 'to take what is going.'

It is rather amusing to note the ideas of those who wrote in the early part of the nineteenth century concerning the practicability of profitably cultivating Dartmoor; ideas which, we venture to believe, the farmer living in that upland region would hardly share. In Cooke's *Topographical Survey of the County of Devon*, published about 1806, are some brief remarks on this subject. Under the heading of 'Hints to the capitalist' we are informed that 'The improvement and cultivation of the Forest of Dartmoor will afford innumerable opportunities for the beneficial exercise of industry and capital. The agriculturist, in particular, will find everything to encourage his exertions.' Since we do not wish to suspect that Mr Cooke was actuated by a desire to mislead when he penned these lines, we can only come to the conclusion that he knew very little about Dartmoor.

Sir Thomas Tyrwhitt, writing about twelve years later in advocacy of the formation of the Plymouth & Dartmoor Railway, sets out with naming the chief object to be aimed at. This was 'to reclaim and clothe with grain and grasses a spacious tract of land, now lying barren, desolate, and neglected; to fill this unoccupied region with an industrious and hardy population.' It is unnecessary to say that although Sir Thomas's railway was made the other part of his programme was uncompleted. Had he consulted some Dartmoor farmer, and listened to his advice, it is certain that he would never have been so sanguine about reclaiming the barren and desolate land as he evidently was.

No ideas such as those held by the visionary of a hundred years ago are entertained by the moorland farmer. He knows that the soil and climate of his uplands are not favourable to the profitable growing of grain, and he puts his land to other uses. In certain spots oats can be grown with advantage, but are usually raised only as dredge corn, that is, they are cut and used as fodder without being threshed. Root crops are also not neglected, turnips often being sown when ground is to be renewed; a crop of oats is taken the next year, and the land is then laid down to pasturage. But Dartmoor turnips are not particularly good; parsnips and carrots do exceedingly well, but turnips are usually not solid. On the smaller farms roots are not grown at all; such as are required for the cattle are bought.

The main obect of Dartmoor farming is to raise cattle, but not to fatten them. When they are of store age, that is, from two to three years old, they are sold to graziers who have rich lands in the in-country, and are there fatted. During winter they are housed and fed on hay, sedge being used for bedding. There is a double economy in this, for not only do the beasts thrive better for the care thus taken of them, but the farmer obtains a quantity of manure.

It is surprising what can be done even on Dartmoor with perseverance. I remember very well when John Hooper enclosed the little farm at Nun's Cross, and he told me not long afterwards that by the time he had got up his walls and his tiny dwelling, and bought a cow, his limited capital had disappeared, or, as his wife more forcibly put it, he possessed no more than 'fourpence hap'ny' to go on with. Yet he did well there. During the later part of his life he was able to sell £100 worth of cattle yearly, which, considering the size of his place, was most satisfactory. But he worked hard, for though not a Dartmoor man born, he possessed all the instincts of one.

Some of the Dartmoor farms are held in connection with others in the in-country, and may be regarded as summer farms. But this is not usual; speaking generally they are farmed by Dartmoor men who spend their lives upon them.

The unlimited pasturage afforded by his large newtakes and the open Forest, on which cattle and sheep can be turned out to graze during summer, are one of the advantages possessed by the

B

Dartmoor farmer; but these will be noticed when we speak of the duties of the moorman.

'Speed the plough' is a motto that is not particularly appropriate on Dartmoor, but everybody will, nevertheless, join in wishing success to the efforts of the sturdy and independent raiser of stock dwelling among its rugged hills.

THE MOORMAN

ALTHOUGH the herdsman's place is generally regarded as being second to that of the tiller of the ground, it cannot be so considered on Dartmoor. The soil and climate militating against the farmer, his operations are restricted, but the moor is all that could be desired as a range for cattle, and consequently the summer pasturing of flocks and herds upon it is, and always has been, of primary importance. Those whose duty it is to take charge of the beasts follow a calling that must therefore be looked upon as the leading one on the moor. They are called moormen, and each is connected with some particular quarter of the Forest, rented from the Duchy, or with one or other of the commons adjacent to it. In the days when the Duchy received cattle to pasture they appointed men to look after them, and these were termed priours. When the present arrangement of farming out the Forest was instituted the office ceased to exist, the modern moorman, who is a tenant and not an employee, taking the priour's place. The moorman is almost always a farmer as well, and consequently the remarks we have made concerning the latter apply equally to him.

A large number of cattle and sheep are annually pastured on the Forest, remaining there from May until September. William Coaker, of Runnage, who rents the east quarter of the Forest, receives probably not less than 2,000 head of cattle each season. For the purpose of looking after this large number he employs several men and boys, each furnished with a horse and dogs. John Edmonds, of South Brent, rents the south quarter, succeeding his father, a fine type of the old moorman. Many a time have we met the latter on the moor, and shall always entertain the most pleasant recollections of him. His fine open face was a sight to behold, and one could listen for hours together to his rich Devon vernacular. Those who have ever heard him in conversation with Richard Eden, another moorman of the south quarter, who has passed away, will not fail to have been impressed with the wonderful force of the Dartmoor doric. 'Upright and down straight,' John Edmonds bore himself in the same manner with every man he met, no matter whether he was a fellow moorman or a 'squire of high degree.' You cannot mention him anywhere round south Dartmoor without hearing expressions of regret that he is no longer seen there.

The north quarter is the largest of the four into which the Forest is divided, and is also much wilder than the others. A considerable portion of it consists of fen, and although the cattle do not range over this, they yet make their way into it along the banks of the streams, where the ground is firm, and consequently the moormen have often very long distances to traverse when in search of them. A duty unknown in the other parts of the moor also devolves upon them here; that of driving the cattle and ponies outside the range of the guns previous to the commencement of artillery practice at the camp on Okehampton Common. This necessitates their being on the Forest very early in the morning, and they have also to hire men to assist them in the work, for which they receive compensation. Among the moormen of the northern part of the Forest the names of Endacott and Edmund Powell are well known. If riding on the bogs of Dartmoor in all weathers should be deemed detrimental to health, no better proof to the contrary could be adduced than Edmund Powell. During his career he has had thousands of head of cattle and sheep in his charge, and if any of them have followed his good example their owners have had nothing to complain of on the score of their laying on flesh. Those who have made the pilgrimage to Cranmere, and who may pride themselves upon having accomplished what is regarded among Dartmoor tourists as a somewhat arduous undertaking, may perhaps learn with some surprise that at one time Edmund Powell was in the habit of visiting it every day. When the limits of the firm ground was reached his pony was tethered to the Ring Rock, and the remainder of the journey was made on foot. Sheep can cross the fen, and it was in order to look after those animals that the dreary morasses were visited.

In the west quarter William Ash, of Horndon, and Henry Palmer, of Redford, or Ruddiver, as he would call it, are familiar figures. The latter rents the extensive common lying within what is known as the hamlet of Willsworthy, within the bounds of which is the wild ravine of Tavy Cleave. The hamlet is in the parish of Peter Tavy, and abuts on the Forest. Redford is a lonely farm at the head of the Willsworthy Brook, an affluent of the Tavy, and here Henry Palmer has lived since he was two years of age. But if you ask him he will tell you he is not without neighbours, and to convince you will point to a farm about half a mile away. He is like another Dartmoor man of my acquaintance, who has lived during his life of sixty years in a secluded valley about a mile and a half in length, and yet does not consider that his house is in such a very lonely situation, for further down are two others, and Princetown is only three miles off.

Samuel Smith, of Hexworthy, is a sub-renter of the south quarter of the Forest, and receives a large number of cattle from the eastern part of the county. He usually gathers them at Bovey Tracey, to which place their owners bring them on certain days at the beginning of the season. He makes four or five journeys there, returning each time with from 50 to 100 head of cattle. When he reaches his home in the Forest the day is far spent, and the animals are placed in one of his fields, where they remain until the following morning, when they are driven to his lair. This is at Green Hill, near the headwaters of the Erme, where is the best pasturage of the south quarter. Here they are visited daily by him, or his man, throughout the season, for beasts seldom stray very far from the spot at which they are first depastured, although free to range. When, however, an animal is found to be missing search is at once made for it, but so well do the moormen understand the habits of the beasts that they can generally find them without much trouble.

Among so many head of cattle, however, it is certain that some will occasionally stray from the lair and be lost. Extended search is then made both 'out auver' and 'in along', meaning on the further side of the ridges moorward, or towards the enclosed country. If it happens that the beasts have strayed to some other part of the moor they will, of course, be seen by another moorman, and their discovery will be easy; but should they make their way to the edge of the moor and get on the roads some difficulty may be experienced in finding them. I remember Samuel Smith —whom I have known for more than a quarter of a century— telling me that he once lost some bullocks from Green Hill, and that they were found some time afterwards in Cornwall. On another occasion a bullock in his charge which had strayed was discovered in the north quarter, and inquiry elicited the fact that the animal had been depastured there in the previous year. Last summer some beasts were missed from the vicinity of Walkham Head, and were found at Bodmin; and some sheep lost from Fur Tor were recovered at Buckland Monachorum. Ponies, or colts, as they are always called by the moormen, range over all parts of the moor, and occasionally make their way by the roads to the in-country. Sometimes animals perish in the mires, but considering the number depastured losses from this are not great. The moormen do not hold themselves responsible for the safety of the animals placed in their charge. A few years ago the owner of a pony which was lost brought an action against the moorman who had care of it to recover its value, and the case was decided in his favour. Since that time all animals have been received on the understanding that they are depastured at the owners' risk. Every reasonable care is taken to see that they do not stray, and search is made for them when they do, and the owner can expect no more. The moormen receive a certain sum per head for bullocks and ponies, and per score for sheep.

Certain spots on the moor are used as places where cattle and sheep are sometimes gathered and counted. There is one on Holne Moor, near Horse Ford, which always goes by the name of

Stascombe Telling-place, in consequence of having been used by a moorman who had charge of some sheep belonging to a farmer of Staddiscombe, in that parish. It is marked by the fragments of an old cross. There is another known as the Drift Court at Coryndon Ball Gate, on the verge of Brent Moor, which was principally used for separating beasts or ponies from a herd, and many others might be named. It is at the time of the drifts—or periodical searchings of the moor for the purpose of ascertaining whether there are any beasts depastured by those possessing no right to do so—that the moorman is busiest. At such times there is often plenty of galloping to do, and the work of gathering the animals is usually accompanied by much shouting, men and horses and dogs all being in a state of great excitement.

Some owners of cattle, possessing rights of pasturage on the moor, do not seek the aid of the moormen, but look after the beasts themselves. In cases where a large number are kept this may be done with advantage, but, speaking generally, it is found that to place them in charge of the moorman is the better plan.

During several years past Scotch cattle have been kept upon the moor. Beside our red Devons they look quite fierce, and their calves are as rough and shaggy as young bears. A herd is kept by Mr Luscombe, in the south part of the moor, and there are also a number on the Okehampton side. A man accustomed to tramping over Dartmoor does not take much notice of the cattle by which he is sometimes surrounded, but it must be confessed that the way in which the Scotch bullocks look at one when you get near them is not very reassuring. On more than one occasion I have had to withdraw from their presence in a very undignified manner. Once a whole herd came rushing down upon—not me, but my dog, but as he ran towards me it amounted to exactly the same thing. Seizing my companion by the hand, I made for a newtake wall that was luckily not far off, and we scrambled over just as the beasts came up. I shall never forget the thundering of their hoofs upon the turf, nor the relief I felt at gaining the shelter of the wall. On another occasion, near Little Hound Tor, a bullock, seemingly tormented by flies, left the herd and came running towards me in a very threatening manner. I hesitated a moment, but seeing that it would be impossible to reach the tor before he would be upon me, I set off down the hill towards the mire above Gallaven Ford, and regardless of the consequences, leapt from one tuft of rushes to another until I had got to some distance from the firm ground. The bullock knew what a mire was as well as I did, and turned away as though disgusted at having wasted his time in seeking an opponent who had not the courage to stand against him. But I am not prepared to say that our own cattle would not have acted in precisely the same way as the Scotch bullocks under similar circumstances. They are certainly not so fierce as their appearance would lead one to suppose.

More than twenty years ago Mr Lamb came to reside at Prince Hall, and introduced Scotch sheep on Dartmoor. Among the runs on the moor he rented Fox Tor farm and Teign Head farm. His death prevented the accomplishment of his plans, but he achieved sufficient to prove that the breed is well adapted to the climate of Dartmoor. Mr Colwill, a grandson of Mr Lamb, still keeps about 1,000 head of these sheep at Fox Tor farm and on Ringmoor Down, but none are now kept at Teign Head. Mr John Pearse, of Kingsett, on Walkhampton Common, also keeps about 100 head. Mr Pearse, in addition to his farming operations, rents the common and takes in cattle to graze.

Dartmoor men can turn their hands to most things, but we do not know that they would be likely to prove very successful on the stage. But while that may be so, the same certainly cannot be said of their sheep. They have proved themselves equal to the strain of a six weeks' run, and won a round of applause each night. In one of the late Mr J. R. Newcombe's pantomimes at the Plymouth Theatre Royal, the animals which Little Bo Peep somehow contrived to lose were represented by a flock of sheep belonging to Mr Lamb, of Prince Hall. During the run of the pantomime the employees of Mr Lamb visited the theatre, and were delighted at the admirable manner in which the curly-coated little Dartmoor actors acquitted themselves.

And now let us accompany the moorman in his search after a bullock which has been reported missing. It is early morning, and as we ride up over Down Ridge, with the dew-sprinkled heather beneath our horses' feet, and the blue sky overhead, in which an invisible songster pours forth his welcome to the day, we begin to think we have never seen the world look more beautiful. Arrived at Skir Ford, Charlie, the moorman's assistant, is sent on to Ryder, with instructions to look about Snowden and Huntingdon, and then to 'get up across an' away vur Arme Poun' ', while we turn our horses' heads towards Ter Hill. When we come in sight of the valley of the Swincombe, below Fox Tor, the moorman reins in his pony, and carefully scrutinises the ground in every direction. 'Bant there,' he says. 'Us'll get along down Black Lane, an' in auver Stall Moor. 'Tis my belief that's where he's gone to; us'll heer zumthin' ov' in into Curnood.' We climb the hill by Fox Tor, and enter Black Lane, which is a narrow strip of firm ground running through the fen. Soon we reach Green Hill, and after a good look around to make sure the bullock has not returned, we cross the Erme and pass up the side of Outer Stall. We can see Erme Pound on the further bank of the stream, but Charlie has not yet arrived. The moorman thinks it is of no use waiting for him; he feels nearly sure that the missing beast is gone 'in along'. 'When Charlie com'th he'll knaw where us be gone,' the moorman says; 'us shan't stap vur ee.' So we ride down by the stone row, carefully scanning Erme Plains as we go, and having satisfied ourselves that the missing beast is not there, turn towards the Yealm, and so on to Watercombe Waste Gate. But we do not pass through, for no sooner do we reach it than we meet Farmer Oatstraw, and he is able to tell us something. 'Zeed'n last night,' he says, in answer to the moorman's inquiry, 'down there in the lane home by Hall. I ope'd the gate there by the bridge an' turn im wi' the doug. You'll vine im roun' by the tar vur zartin.' And so we do, or at least Charlie does, for he comes riding up a few minutes after and we send him down to make the search. When we leave the animal at Green Hill we venture to hint at the possibility of its again going 'in along'. 'An' if he dith,' says the moorman, 'us'll hev to vetch'n, that's all.'

The Farmer   Mr and Mrs Cleave and child at the door of Higher Meripit.
Photograph by Robert Burnard, 4 August 1892

The Labourer The Forest I[n]
Hexworthy. The board over t[he]
door is the one referred to in 'T[he]
Labourer'. The inn is now mu[ch]
larger and quite different in eve[ry]
way. Photograph by Robert B[ur]
nard, 9 October 1888

The Newtake Wall Builder Jon[as]
Coaker, the Dartmoor poet a[nd]
wall builder. Photograph by Robe[rt]
Burnard, taken about 1876

THE LABOURER

THE work of the Dartmoor labourer is in some respects of a different character from that which his fellow in the lowland districts has to perform, though this is perhaps not so much the case where unskilled labour is concerned. But a good deal of what he has to do requires special skill, and these duties form no part of the work of the ordinary rural labourer. Of such are the clearing of rocky ground, the building, or repairing of newtake walls, or the cutting of peat, each of more or less importance. With these, however, we propose to deal separately, and for the present shall confine our remarks chiefly to what may be considered as unskilled labour. This, though not differing greatly from the same kind of work in other places, is yet performed under conditions that are not the same, and therefore appear to be worthy of notice.

In the times when the severity of the Dartmoor climate was ignored, and it was sought to prove that ordinary farming operations could be profitably conducted on the moor, it was made to appear that a new era was dawning for the moorland labourer. He was henceforth to be employed in a precisely similar manner to the farmer's man who worked in the beautiful country he saw stretching from the foot of his native hills. He was to become familiar with the use of the reaping-hook and the flail, and was to obtain nearly all he required from land he had hitherto regarded as being capable of affording nothing more than summer pasturage for cattle and sheep. His cot was to be embosomed in trees, and around him he was to see only smiling fields. These were the hopes he was expected to entertain by those who, less than a century ago, were going to work such a mighty change; a prospect over which people grew enthusiastic, and which bards sung in hopeful expectation, as though there were more to awaken

27

the muse in a crop of turnips than in the primeval desolation of the moor. But the thousand cots that were to dot the sward, and the fields of ripening grain, were but a mirage, and took no more real shape than the mist that wreathes the tors. That the labourer was disappointed at the failure to realise what was hoped for is not probable. He never believed in the schemes that were set on foot; he knew too well what Dartmoor was.

Those who worked for the earlier of the modern 'improvers' of the moor have, of course, long passed away, but there are those living who very well remember the later attempts to introduce farming on a large scale on Dartmoor. I am acquainted with one who for some time was employed at Prince Hall when that estate was in the possession of Mr G. W. Fowler, who commenced operations there about 1846. Some of the workmen, and among them my acquaintance, lived at a considerable distance from Prince Hall, and being able to return to their homes at the end of the week only, a large loft was assigned to them as a sleeping apartment. According to my informant the crops of grain that were raised were far from satisfactory, and had they even been good would have shown a pecuniary loss, the cost of manuring the ground being so great. With his root crops Mr Fowler appears to have been a little more successful; at all events he had quantity, if not quality, for my acquaintance describes the turnips that he grew as 'proper great benders'. The farm buildings were on a very complete scale, there being, according to what the Dartmoor man used to say, only one thing lacking. This, he would tell you, in playful irony, was a cider press; if that were added, he said, the buildings would be equal to those to be found on the most superior in-country farm. Mr Fowler informed the writer's father that although he had lost a considerable sum of money at Prince Hall, he did not regret his experiments there. They had interested him for several years, and had satisfied him that operations on Dartmoor, if they were to be profitable, must be in the direction of the formation of pastures.

Since the attempts to turn the moor into a second South Hams have been abandoned, certain kinds of work that the labourer had formerly to do he is not now often required to perform. The paring and burning of the surface, the first step towards bringing coarse land into a state of cultivation, is a work in which he is at present seldom employed, but at one time it afforded him much occupation. It is known as spading, and was usually paid for by the perch, or yard, as it is more often called. The late Richard Cleave, of Hexworthy, once told me that his father spaded many acres of land for the farmer at Fox Tor, in the early part of the last century, and that he was paid $4\frac{1}{2}$d a yard for the work.

Although the draining of bogs on the moor has never been undertaken to any considerable extent, it is at the same time a work to which the labourer is not entirely a stranger. Those who pasture cattle on the Forest have at times found it to their advantage to endeavour to render them less dangerous by draining their worst parts. This is done by cutting a deep and narrow trench, or gutter, as the Dartmoor man always calls it, through the mire. The work, however, is usually only temporary in its effects, for the trenches soon fill, and the swamp becomes as bad as ever.

As we still call Dartmoor a Forest, notwithstanding that it lost its status as such several hundred years ago, it is only reasonable to expect that we should find foresters there. And in this we shall not be disappointed, though it is true we shall be able to count them on the fingers of one hand. But the moor having been in a great measure stripped of the few sylvan honours it once possessed, and the herds of deer which formerly ranged over it being reduced to occasional stragglers from Exmoor, the work of the forester is all but gone, and the present representatives of the craft are consequently sufficient. In a cottage on Gobbet Plain, above Hexworthy, lives Edward Caunter, who finds work for his hands to do in the woods and plantations of Brimpts. His dwelling stands in a situation that was certainly not dictated by a regard to shelter, for it is exposed to every wind that sweeps across the moor. But its occupier—Ned, as he is always called—takes no notice of 'thackey'. With strong walls and a sufficiency of 'turve' he can bid defiance to the winter storm, and is as comfortable when seated by his hearth as though his cottage stood in some secluded valley in the in-country. Ned is a hewer of wood, working on the Duchy plantations, as his father, George Caunter, did before him, and as it is probable his son, who bears his own Christian name, will do after him. At all events the latter works with his father, and in the two the calling of the forester survives on Dartmoor. It is not, however, the sturdy oak that they bring to the ground. One finds few of those on the moor; but there is an abundance of fir at Brimpts, and this tree it is that chiefly falls before them.

Edward Caunter is getting a bit grey now, like the rocks that lie scattered near his dwelling. He is 'terrible crippled up with rheumatics,' too, though I can remember the time when he had only to hear 'The Soldier's Joy' played on a comb or the concertina, and an effect was produced upon him as wonderful as that caused by a snake-charmer's flute. He would spring into the middle of the kitchen, and favour those present with a specimen of his abilities as a step-dancer, and prove himself a nimble performer, too, notwithstanding that he carried about seven pounds weight of leather and iron on his feet. But many years have passed since then, and now Ned's dancing days are over.

I was once engaged with his father in a piece of work of which we were both rather proud. About twenty-five years ago, when at Hexworthy, something was said one day about the state of the signboard over the door of the Forest Inn, which happened to be rather the worse for wear. It would certainly have puzzled a stranger to decipher the legend it bore unless he were quite close to it, and it was considered that the time had arrived when it should be repainted. But here a difficulty arose. There was no painter within several miles, and the Dartmoor men did not pretend to the possession of any artistic ability. Neither did I, the execution of certain large subjects in distemper and exhibited only behind the footlights being the utmost to which I had attained; but I neverthless signified my readiness to undertake the work. Then it struck Richard Cleave, the landlord, that such an artist ought to have a larger field for the display of his talents. The present signboard was too small. He would have a new one; and it was here that the forester became associated with me in the work. Uncle George, as he was always called, was spoken to on the matter. After much consultation the size of the signboard was determined upon, and the old man set to work. When he had finished I commenced. The colours had previously been obtained from Ashburton, and it was not long before I had the gratification of seeing my painting hung in the Forest of Dartmoor. Whether I had at the time any hopes that the sign would immortalise me I do not now remember, but very few years proved how vain such would have been. Uncle George's part of the work still remains, but the Dartmoor weather proved too much for mine. The brush of another artist has since been laid upon the board, and has blotted out my colours for ever.

It was quite by chance that the Forest Inn received its appropriate name. The late Mr Cleave told me that when he decided to apply for a licence for the house many years ago, he intended calling it the 'Foresters' Arms', but a few minutes before making his application at Tavistock he was dissuaded from this by a friend whom he happened to meet there, and who suggested the name it now bears.

Although there is little wood on Dartmoor itself, there are many villages on its borders clothed with coppices, and in these such labourers as live anywhere near them will sometimes find work. This consists in felling the trees forming the copse, and stripping them of their bark, which work is termed ripping. The wood is often sold for firewood, and the bark goes to the tanneries.

The work of the thatcher is distinct from that of the ordinary labourer, as it, of course, requires a special knowledge; but we mention it here as being the most convenient place. But even in the Dartmoor country he finds less employment year by year, as slate roofs, or corrugated iron ones for outhouses, are now becoming general. For covering ricks, however, he is still in request, and that he may not be short of reed, a little rye is grown on the moor. The thatch on the roofs of some old buildings is of an amazing thickness, consequent upon fresh layers having been added from time to time during a considerable period. From a building at Beardon, a farm not far from Lydford village, the thatch was found on its removal some months ago to be no less than five feet in thickness. Some thatchers are very clever at their work, and pride themselves upon its neatness. One who was particularly noted was Edmund Fry, of Lydford, who also made for himself a name as a sheep-shearer, being the winner of several prizes. He lost his life while following his employment. In January of the present year he fell from the roof of a cottage at Lydford and was immediately killed.

But the general labourer on Dartmoor finds perhaps as much employment on the roads as in any direction, while a considerable number are also engaged, particularly during the winter, on work in connection with the Devonport leat. The latter is conducted for a considerable distance across the Forest, and also through Walk-hampton Common, and during the season of frost and snow requires much attention in order to prevent it from becoming blocked. It is necessary to employ gangs of men for this work, and thus the Dartmoor labourer is afforded a means of earning wages at a time of the year when he might otherwise find it difficult to do so in his own immediate neighbourhood.

Although the Dartmoor labourer may not earn so much as his fellow in the towns, there can be no doubt that he leads a far happier life. He has less money, it is true, but he has also less expenses, while the nature of his surroundings and his employment breed in him a certain spirit of independence. In place of a single room for himself and wife and family, looking out on begrimed roofs and a dirty back court, he has a little cottage and a garden, a rick of peat for his hearth, plenty of pure air, and seeing nothing but what Nature has made, looks only upon that which has beauty. His food is plain, but he is probably the better for that, so long as he has enough of it. As a rule he is not dissatisfied with his lot, although he naturally wishes to better it, as he would do were he a hundred times better off. Speaking generally, he appreciates such advantages as changed times have given him over his predecessors, and also such as his children have gained. There are exceptions, of course. It was not so very long since that, at the Forest Inn, a labourer, on being asked by his companions what he thought of the Education Act, gave it as his opinion that 'this heer free ederication bant no good to nobody'.

Not infrequently the Dartmoor labourer lays down the beginnings of a little farm. There are difficulties at first, but these are overcome in time. His rent is low; the poultry, by skilful management, are made to pay a good part of it, and by-and-by, when he milks his first cow, there is not only no need for any of it to come out of his wages, but he can commence to put by a little for his second cow. Brought up on the moor, he knows exactly what it is capable of, and has, therefore, reason to hope for success. He knows he cannot perform impossibilities, and therefore does not attempt to turn the desert into a garden. He makes the best of Dartmoor as he finds it.

THE NEWTAKE
WALL BUILDER

ONE of the first things the early Dartmoor settler had to do was to enclose the land he had marked out for his farm, and consequently the building of walls was an occupation that preceded all other forms of labour. When his successor enclosed more land, in accordance with a custom of the Forest that gave him the right to do so, more walls were also necessary, and the building of them thus became a part of the labourer's work. The custom of making these additions was called landyoke, landbote, or newtake, and by the latter name these parcels of enclosed land are now, and have for long, been known. It does not, however, appear that the right to form enclosures was acted upon to any very great extent, for down to the latter part of the eighteenth century the newtakes were few in number, and wall building could therefore never have been an occupation demanding much of the labourer's attention. But at the period named, and during the first part of the nineteenth century, all this was altered. With the rage for enclosing, the newtake wall builder came to the front, and for many years he found constant employment on the Forest.

It must not, however, be supposed that the erection of long lines of walls has greatly altered the face of the moor. Enclosing land did not often mean the reclaiming of it. The latter was, of course, intended by those 'improvers' who had acquired leases of large tracts, but the results of their agricultural experiments over a small area not being encouraging the surface of their immense enclosures—they are not newtakes in the true sense of the word, though always so-called—was left undisturbed. When it was at length realised that Dartmoor could not be profitably cultivated, and that to enclose land was worse than useless, the newtake wall builder found much of his occupation gone, and at a later period he became still less in request. This was when the question of interference with the commoners' rights forced itself upon the attention of those who desired the preservation of Dartmoor. These rights had been ignored by the enclosers, as well as by those who had granted them leases in the land. A large extent of good pasturage was taken from the commoner, and had the system been allowed to continue he would in a few years have been left only the worst parts of the Forest on which to depasture his beasts. The enclosing of land within its bounds having been stopped, consequent upon the representations that were made on this subject, it is only when already existing newtakes are divided, or when walls require to be repaired, that the builder is needed. This is, of course, not of everday occurence, but it has occasionally to be done, and consequently the earliest form of labour that the settler engaged in is still to be witnessed on the Forest.

The newtake walls are formed of stones piled to a height of about four or five feet, and in some cases more, no mortar, not even turf, being used. The material lay ready to the builder's hand; all he had to do was to collect the stones, and upon the size of those, of course, depended the character of his wall. They are sometimes seen to be so small that the wall has little stability, and in some cases the spaces between them are such as to cause the latter to present almost the appearance of a network of stones. In the moorman's language : one can see daylight through them. When the stones lying around him were large, a solid wall was the result, but the earlier builder never went out of his way to obtain his material, nor did he ever break any stones or attempt to shape them. In later years, however, a different plan was adopted. Small stones were generally discarded, and the larger ones that were employed were roughly squared. One of the first to introduce this style of newtake wall building on Dartmoor was John Bishop, of Swincombe, whose work, as he would tell you, was 'ordained to stand'.

Examples of the old and the new styles may be seen on the

road between Two Bridges and Cherrybrook Bridge, below Smith Hill. On one side are the enclosures belonging to Prince Hall, the wall of which was built many years ago, the stones composing it being comparatively small, particularly in places. On the other side is Muddy Lakes, a modern enclosure, and the wall—one of John Bishop's building—is formed of huge blocks of granite fitted closely together. Bishop had great faith in the powers of the crowbar, or 'bar ire' as he called it. Asked on one occasion how he contrived to get such immense stones in their places, he replied, 'Aw, 'tis surprisin' what you can do with a laiver or two.' As a means of conveying stones to any required spot there was nothing in his estimation equal to the sled, or sledge. He was very fond of praising the performances of a certain pony with one of these carriages. 'He belonged to my vayther,' he used to say, 'an' wudden no more'n vourteen, or vourteen an' a half, an' I've a zeed'n shift a stone up dree tin wight 'pon a sledge.' When asked if he really meant to say that a pony of such a size could draw so heavy a weight, he would answer, 'Ees; 'pon a sledge, I tell you.'

A part of the moor in which a great many modern newtakes may be seen is South Tawton Common. Here, on the slope of Cosdon, in the neighbourhood of Ramsleigh Mine, are numerous enclosures, some of them having only been formed within the past three or four years. This common is not in the Forest, and our remarks relative to new enclosures were in regard to that portion of the moor only. They are, however, equally applicable to all the commons surrounding the Forest so far as the rights of commoners are concerned.

The newtake wall builder, gathering his material on the scene of his labours, cleared much of the ground as he proceeded with his work. Such loose stones as he did not use were often gathered into heaps as may be seen in many of the newtakes today. In Fox Tor newtake are a number of such heaps, composed principally of small stones, and in one of the enclosures of Hexworthy is a collection of larger blocks built up with such regularity on the surface of a flat rock as almost to leave the impression that the pile was intended to serve some particular purpose. Another plan, and one perhaps more often adopted by the builder for disposing of his surplus stones, was to considerably increase the thickness of his walls in the corners of his enclosures, where they are sometimes seen five or six feet in breadth. On Brousen Tor farm, in the parish of Peter Tavy, this device is particularly noticeable in one of the fields, where the wall is of such extraordinary thickness and height throughout as to suggest the remains of some ancient stronghold. Indeed, in that locality there are many walls of a height far above that usually seen. On the verge of Cudlipp Town Down, under White Tor, this is particularly the case.

Eighty years ago another method was suggested for disposing of the stones that encumbered the ground. It appears in the notes to Cottle's poem of 'Dartmoor', but as it has not been adopted, it is to be presumed that the moor labourer has never heard of it. As he is not in the habit of reading poetry, this is not strange. We will let Mr Cottle, who, by the way, did not altogether share in the general enthusiasm of his time respecting the agricultural capabilities of the moor, unfold his plan himself. He says: 'One great impediment, however, to the cultivation of Dartmoor will arise from the immense number of large stones, with which nearly the whole surface of the land is closely covered. To remove them wholly, or to gather them into heaps (like the stones in a common field after manure), would be almost impracticable. The thought occurred to me on the spot that the most frugal and effectual way to get rid of these stones would be by digging deep holes immediately adjoining, and then by burying them.' What would the Dartmoor man think of that? Mr Cottle very modestly confesses that this brilliant idea may have been suggested by Dr Stukeley's supposition with regard to the stones at Stonehenge, which he thought may have been forced up an inclined plane and dropped down into the holes prepared for them. Mr Cottle does not say whether his plan was to extend to the tors of Dartmoor. If so, it is very fortunate it was not adopted, otherwise such grand piles as Hey Tor or Great Mis Tor might now be hidden underground.

We have said that the newtake wall builder never went out of his way to search for material. But he often did to avoid obstacles that presented themselves as his work proceeded. When a big rock happened to lie in his path, if he could not carry his wall over it he took it round it. The consequence was that, like a certain street referred to by Mark Twain, it was anything but straight. One may stand in places and look upon an old wall wriggling like a huge serpent over the heath. It is not probable that the builder had ever heard the axiom that there is no beauty in straight lines, but he certainly carried out his work as though he had.

Sometimes the wall will suddenly leave what may be supposed to be its true line, and, making an outward sweep, return to it a few yards further on, a semi-circular projection being thus formed. The object of this is not apparent to the ordinary observer, but it will in most cases be found that this little excresence has a spring rising upon it. The builder has discovered it near the line of his wall, and has carried the latter around it in order that his enclosure may be supplied with water. Often the wall sweeps inwards instead of outwards, and the area it partly encircles is larger than in the preceding case. This is usually seen in the wall of enclosures on the verge of the moor, the object of such an arrangement being to form convenient spots in which to gather cattle or ponies. They are, in fact, the 'telling-places' to which we have referred in our remarks on the moorman, and are sometimes also known as 'courts.' It is, however, probable that these places were not all designed for the purpose to which the moorman puts them, but that they had originally some connection with the deer. The Court Rolls relating to the moor show that persons were often fined for suffering the walls and gates to be in a ruinous condition.

In places a wide space may be seen between the newtakes, and these are called strolls. Their chief purpose is to allow of cattle passing to some stream, but they also afford them some degree of shelter during rough weather. There is little doubt that at one time these strolls were more numerous than at present. The land-grabber is responsible for their disappearance. He saw how easy it was to form them into newtakes, two walls only being required to enclose the space, instead of three or four, and regardless of any other consideration he converted them to his own use.

Another plan of the land-grabber was to form an enclosure at a little distance from any others, and, awaiting his opportunity, connect it with them by means of a couple of walls. By adopting this plan he was able to acquire a much larger piece of ground than he would otherwise have been suffered to take without objection being raised. Detached newtakes may yet be met with that were evidently formed with this intention. It must not, however, be assumed that this was so in every instance; in some cases the space between the newtakes will be found to be on the line of some old track, which had the enclosure been joined to the others would have been obstructed. Instances of paths being blocked are never found among the older enclosures. It is only where the modern land-grabber's hand is seen that rights-of-way have been interfered with.

In some instances enclosures have been formed on the site of ancient hut settlements, the new wall being raised on the ruins of the older one. The newtake wall builder cared nothing about the rude stone remains of the moor further than that they furnished him with excellent material for his work, and to his charge must be laid the destruction of numberless hut circles and kistvaens, and other objects of a similar character.

Newtakes are sometimes found in an unfinished condition, the enclosers having apparently arrived at the conclusion that it was not worth while to proceed with the work. Lengths of wall, often in a dilapidated state, are also seen where attempts have been made to enclose commons, the Irishman's Wall near Belstone being a notable example. According to an account which I gathered in the locality many years ago, those employed in the building of it, who were all from the sister isle, astonished the people of the moor by their utter contempt for boots and stockings. But they in their turn were probably astonished when one day they found a great part of their work destroyed. The men of Belstone and Okehampton had no notion of having their commons enclosed, and so they threw the wall down. What became of the Irishmen my informant did not know, but he expressed the opinion that their own country was a much more suitable place for them than Dartmoor. 'What could um expect to do 'pon the moor,' he said, 'wi' nort to their vait?'

Women have sometimes been employed as newtake wall builders. A great part of the wall above the western side of Hound Tor Combe, and northward of Hemsworthy Gate, was built by two women, and when John Hooper enclosed his little farm at Nun's Cross, some thirty-three years ago, his wife, as I have heard her say more than once, assisted him to erect the walls. Her part consisted more particularly of gathering stones and bringing them to her husband. Other similar instances might be mentioned, and are not so strange when we remember that on Dartmoor women have worked in mines, cut peat, and engaged in all kinds of labour usually performed by men.

Every newtake has got a name. Some of these are very ancient, as existing records of the Forest show, but by far the greater number are modern. And this is the case with Dartmoor names generally. Not a few are of Celtic or Saxon derivation, but most of them have been given to places and objects by the moormen in quite recent times. For many years I have been collecting place-names for a dictionary of Dartmoor, and have succeeded in obtaining a very large number, some three or four thousand of which have never yet appeared in print. These show me that modern names predominate to a very considerable extent.

In this connection reference may be made to a name that appears on maps, and is now often spoken of as Newlake. It should however, be Newtake, and is the name of a hill, so called from its proximity to the enclosures of Teign Head, which were formed in the latter part of the eighteenth century. It is not improbable that the engraver of the early nineteenth-century map is responsible for the error.

One of the most noted of newtake wall builders, next to John Bishop, was Jonas Coaker, well-known as the Dartmoor poet. It was in the days when men seriously believed they could profitably cultivate Dartmoor that Jonas turned his attention to the work so that he did not lack employment. He was very fond of the occupation and followed it for some time. But the days were coming when the 'improver' was to find out his mistake. When they did arrive, and the work of the newtake wall builder was not as it was, Jonas found something else to do.

One may still see the builder at work, occasionally, but it is satisfactory to know that he is only employed by the farmer now.

SWALING

IT is a beautiful day in September, and as you enter upon the commons from the narrow lane bordered by grey walls, in the crevices of which tiny ferns find a congenial home, you think you have never seen anything so fresh and fair. Far below is a narrow valley, where trees hide from view the stream that is forcing its way through the shady depths to the sunshine beyond. Above the trees are pastures, and fields that have just been reaped, with sheltering hedgerows, green lanes and old farmhouses. Further up the hedges give place to walls, and patches of gorse are seen in the enclosures. Outside the walls is the open common stretching upward to the tor, and upon this your eye is resting. The river valley and the farm lands have beauties to which you are not oblivious, but they are passed by for the moment, for the bloom of the heather has purpled the hill, and it is now the most charming feature of a picture in which it is always a striking one.

When September again comes round you once more pass up the lane between the lichen-stained walls. The little ferns still grow in their crevices, as though there were no such thing as the winter storm, but blue skies and sunshine ever. When you pass through the moor gate you look down upon the trees in the valley, and the meadows, and the stubble fields. You see the stone walls, and the gorse dotting the rough ground that they enclose. All is as it was twelve months ago except the hill that rises from the enclosures. That no longer wears a robe of purple, and the picture has lost much of its beauty. You pass across the common to the hill, and you find where the heather grew only blackened stems and short grass. Fire has destroyed the mantle on which you delighted to gaze, and you cannot repress a feeling of sorrow at seeing it shorn of its glory. You speak of it to a passing moorman,

42

Swaling Mr Jim Endacott, then Duchy Reeve, swaling near Post Bridge between the wars while his pony, Gerry, stands nearby. Mr Endacott was the son of the moorman of that name mentioned in the chapter 'The Moorman'

Peat Cutting Cutting peat in 1912

Peat Cutting Cutting peat in 1913: the figure is thought to be Lewis White, of Lower Meripit

Peat Cutting Bringing down the peat from Whitehorse Hill *c.* 1903. The carts are
on the Batworthy road by the Round Pound, and Kes Tor is in the background. The
leading figure is the moorman, Mr William Endacott, and his son Jim, then about 14
is in charge of the last cart in the line

and he tells you the ground has been swaled, or, in other words, that the furze and heather have been intentionally burnt.

However much the destruction of the covering of Dartmoor is to be deplored, swaling is absolutely necessary. Were this growth suffered to remain undisturbed of what value would the pasturage be? It may rejoice the soul of the lover of the beautiful in Nature to look upon a rolling sea of purple, but would he wish that Dartmoor should serve no other purpose. I remember when the heather grew to such a height on Holne Moor that it brushed my feet when riding through it; and in places it was much higher. The spectacle in the early autumn was a gorgeous one, though it no doubt appealed to the moorman in a different way. Its only use was to afford cover for black cock; a thing to be desired, perhaps, from the sportsman's point of view, but giving little satisfaction to those who needed the common as a grazing ground. The great tract of land was benefiting nobody, and so the heather was burnt, and cattle and sheep and ponies have since roamed over it at will, finding keep where there formerly was none. That considerations of profit should be placed before everything can on no account be admitted. Indeed, in many instances those of a merely sentimental character are of far more importance; they often elevate the mind, while the former not only does not do this, but has a tendency to operate in a contrary direction. But there are occasions when sentiment must be content to stand on one side; it cannot expect to be listened to when it would inflict a loss upon the community.

Were the benefits derived from swaling of slight importance only, and did the practice actually deface the moor, it would be difficult to say one word in its favour. But such is not the case. The value of Dartmoor as a summer grazing ground is considerable, and nothing that contributes to the excellency and extent of its pasturage can be neglected. By burning the heather the grass is allowed to grow, and abundant keep is provided for the thousands of head of cattle that are annually taken charge of by the moormen. This, of course, robs the moor of some of its beauty, but it is in no way defacing, as the grass springs up very quickly.

That a necessity exists for the practice all who possess a love of the beautiful will lament, but there would be very much less cause for regret if the farmer and the moorman were alone accountable for the swaling on the moor.

Much of the heather is destroyed by irresponsible persons. It is an unfortunate fact that there are individuals to whom the charms of Nature do not appeal. Such sometimes find their way to Dartmoor, though why they should do so is a mystery, and, being unable to appreciate what they see there, find enjoyment in doing as much damage as they can. They admire a big blaze far more than the purple garb in which the old moor sometimes wraps itself; the one is exciting and is suitable to their instincts; to enjoy the other requires taste. And so they set fire to the heather, and, more likely than not, on some part of the common where the ground is useless as pasture, and which the moorman would never think of burning. Of what advantage, for instance, would it be to him to destroy the heather and the gorse and fern covering a rocky hillside over which cattle would never range? Only those tracts of land that will afford pasturage when they are cleared of such growth are swaled by him, for he has no motive in burning beyond providing keep for the beasts in his care. The farmer and the moorman cannot be accused of injuring the appearance of the moor, at least not to any considerable extent. If swaling were left entirely to them—and they alone have a right to do it—its effects would not be such as to afford ground for very serious complaint. Dartmoor is so large that those who seek it for its beauties, those to whom fine scenery is a real delight, need not fear that it will be stripped of its purple and its gold by those who dwell upon it. They may well be content to share it with the herdsman, for there is enough for each.

During the past few years more attention has been directed to the practice of burning the heather and furze than was formerly the case. Parish councils have very wisely imposed a time limit to swaling, and this cannot but have beneficial results. By the Whitchurch Council it is only permitted from 1 to 31 March, and the

Mary Tavy Council have made a similar regulation. Those who know how much some of the border commons have been injured in appearance by young persons and children burning the heather and furze merely for the sake of amusement, or in a spirit of mischief, will not only agree as to the necessity of such a restriction, but would welcome the prohibition of swaling by any except those possessing grazing rights, and over a certain age. The month of March, or the earlier part of April, is the proper time for the work, yet I have known whole acres of heather to be burnt in the autumn. The action that has been taken has, however, stopped this practice, and it is also to be hoped that it will prove effective in other directions. We will hope for more; that indiscriminate burning of the heather and gorse on Dartmoor may cease not so much on account of being prohibited, but because of the book of Nature becoming more widely read, and of a fuller appreciation of the beauties she displays. It is sad to see only blackened stems where golden furze might be, or heather slopes laid waste, when no useful purpose has been served by the work of destruction. At the present time the steep banks of Crazy Well Pool, on Walk-hampton Common, boast scarcely a heather plant; fire has denuded them of their covering, and it will be long ere the deep waters again reflect the purple bloom that once clothed them. This is not the work of the moorman, for so precipitous are the banks that not even a sheep could descend them, and such herbage as has sprung up there is of no more service than the growth it has displaced. The destruction of what but lately gave so much beauty to the Pool was a wanton act, and one which cannot be too strongly condemned.

While the needless burning of the covering of Dartmoor is to be deplored mostly for the reason that a scarcity of heather would detract from its appearance, the sportsman has also some ground of complaint. The farmer and moorman is always more or less a Nimrod, and can usually enjoy ' a rin wi' the har-yers' with the best of them. Their instincts would therefore lead them to avoid, if possible, burning the heather in such places, or at such times, as might interfere with sport, for your genuine Dartmoor man is always pleased when he is able to inform the Master of the pack that he 'knaws by a hare'. But no such judgement is exercised by the person who sets fire to it mischievously, not only because he knows nothing whatever about such a matter, but because he cares less.

The effect at night of a large tract of heather burning is very striking, especially if the fires happen to be near a tor or a stream. There is something weird about the scene when the red glare is thrown upon the rocks or reflected in the dark waters, seen one moment, and the next hidden by the dense clouds of smoke. Only a rushing sound and the crackling of stems is heard; there is no loud roar, and at even a short distance the flames seem to give forth no sound. This adds much to its strangeness; it is like a silent sea of fire rolling away into the darkness beyond.

There is one danger that may arise from the burning of heather during a hot summer, and which has been pointed out by the Rev. E. Spencer. The peat is then so parched and dry that there is a possibility of the fire extending to it. This, when smoke and flame are no more seen, continues to smoulder, and carbonic acid gas[1] is thrown off; the rambler approaching the spot from a direction opposite to that from which the wind is blowing runs considerable risk. Such an occurrence is fortunately rare, for a period of drought sufficiently long to cause the peat to become dry to any considerable depth is not often witnessed on Dartmoor.

The old moor is chiefly indebted for the colourings of its summer garb to the bloom of the bell heather and the ling, and for the golden fringe adorning this purple mantle to the gorse, growing principally on its borders, and to the paler yellow of the broom. In places the mantle is slashed with white. This is away where the heather does not grow, but gives place to the waving bog-grass and the cotton rush.

The moor has put on this garb now. As I write I can see the

[1] The old name for carbon dioxide.

purple and the gold, turning the stern, tor-capped hills into things of beauty. I do not fear that they will ever be stripped, if the vandal does not bring his torch upon the waste. They will not harm much if we leave them to the moorland dweller, but it is sad to think there are some who could lay those slopes bare without scruple. For such the glories of Nature have no message.

PEAT CUTTING

AMONG the rights possessed by the Dartmoor commoner that of turbary was at one time of considerable importance. Under changed conditions, however, the use of peat as a fuel is now restricted to a much smaller area than formerly, but in the more remote farmhouses its value continues to be recognised. The peat stack is still a familiar object near many a moorland dwelling, and the aroma arising from the fire that is fed from it yet salutes the nostrils of the rambler as he passes by. Deprived of many of Nature's bounties the Dartmoor man has nevertheless a few compensating advantages, and excellent fuel, to be obtained for the labour of cutting it, and in any quantity, is not among the least of these.

This right of turbary he has exercised for centuries, peat until recent years being his only fuel. The procuring of this has always formed part of the labourer's summer employment, and more than one place-name is indicative of this branch of his work. Thus the Turbary of Alberysheved, between the South Teign and the headwaters of the Bovey, mentioned in the Forest perambulation of 1240, though it appears to have afterwards lost that name, was yet known in later times by one connecting it with the cutting of peat, for in the survey of 1609, where it is described as a fenny place, it is called Turf Hill. The occurrence of the name White, as in White Tor, White Lake, White Barrow, and in other connections, is supposed, with excellent reason, to be due to the presence of the tinners on the moor, as it most certainly is in White Works; and there can be no doubt that Black, also frequently met with, had reference, in some cases at least, to the peat. The Dartmoor man never speaks of it as such: he calls it either 'turve' or 'black 'ood', i.e., black wood. And so we have the Blackwood Path on Ugborough Moor, and Black Lane, leading

48

to the extensive ties at Brook's Head, in the north quarter of the Forest, and others. We have also Stooky Moor, which evidently has reference to the small piles of cut peat, known as 'stooks', and Turver, on Amicombe Hill, where the peat is of great depth. Many useful tracks on the moor originated with the peat-cutter; and I know also of clapper bridges the erection of which are traceable to him.

Much peat has been cut on Dartmoor other than for the purpose of supplying the dwellers in that region with fuel. Seven centuries ago the tinners were permitted to take it for the fusion of their ore, and it is still used by the miner today, though not for smelting. In the last century large quantities were consumed at the mines in Mary Tavy, particularly at Wheal Betsy on Black Down, where lead was smelted. This was obtained at Walkham Head, about five miles from the mine, where peat is still cut by the farmer. In the *Handbook for Devon*, published in 1879, the rambler is told that he will find near the source of the Walkham eleven upright blocks of granite, 'which he may spend an hour in sketching as a Druidical monument; but they are probably the pillars which once supported a shed at an old tin stream-work.' The visitor might well be pardoned for such a mistake seeing that there have been those who imagined they saw the work of the Druids in rock basins and holed stones; he would at least not commit the error of regarding that which Nature had wrought as being formed by the hand of man. The suggestion that the pillars—few of which are now standing—marked the site of a mine shed is, however, not quite correct; they really supported the roof of a building erected by the adventurers of Wheal Betsy for the purpose of storing peat in, and which was known as the Turf House. Considerable quantities of peat were cut during each summer, and this, instead of being brought away when dried, was stored on the spot, and fetched from the mine as required.

One of my Dartmoor acquaintances, John Burn, of Mary Tavy, who died about three years ago, remembered very well when the building was in use. He lived for some time at Waps-

D

worthy, and was familiar with the neighbourhood of Walkham Head, and, indeed, all that part of the moor westward of the West Dart and the West Ockment. John Burn once performed the feat of driving a horse and cart laden with rushes from the branch of the Tavy rising to the south of Cut Hill to the springs of the Walkham. The fen is here of such a nature that, except in a dry season, it is not easy to cross it on foot. I have found it barely passable even in summer after a few days' rain.

The peat beds of Dartmoor have also attracted the notice of others than the tinners. In quite recent times they have been the scene of various enterprises having for their object either the cutting and rapidly preparing of the peat for fuel, or the obtaining of certain products from it, but they have all been abandoned. The latest attempt to find a commercial value for it was made in 1901, when arrangements were entered into to take over the disused works at Rattle Brook Head, built by a company formed about twenty-five years ago. The scheme seemed to give promise of success, for the peat instead of being placed upon the market as such, was to be carbonised. This was to be effected by subjecting it to great pressure between plates heated to a high degree. The result of the experiment appeared to be satisfactory, but the venture was nevertheless not proceeded with. It was found that Nature had been anticipated only to a certain extent. The compressed peat bore a great resemblance to coal, and possibly possessed most of its properties, but the combustion was too rapid to lead to the expectation of its being profitably employed. Whether, as a result of discoveries, peat may yet become an article of commerce remains to be seen. At present the Dartmoor man has not been beaten.

If we would learn something of the nature of the peat cutter's work we cannot do better than bear him company to the tie, or pit, from which he procures it. He is going 'up along to Skir', where generations of 'old men' have gone for their fuel before him, and where it is still to be obtained in abundance. His labour has sometimes been described by those having little knowledge of it as digging, but such it certainly is not. The process is entirely one of cutting, and the tools used—irons, as the Dartmoor man calls them—are very sharp. These are three in number: the budding-iron, the long knife (or slicer), and the turf-iron. The use of them we shall learn when our companion commences his work.

Having gained the summit of the hill, perhaps not quite so speedily as we might have done, for we have found it impossible not to pause now and again to look back upon the widening view of the Forest, we pass down the slight descent to the Wobrook. Crossing this tributary of the Dart—here only a small stream— we follow the peat track for a short distance, and then make our way up the slope of Skir to the left. Speedily the hills and tors, which we lost sight of when we descended to the fording-place, come once more into view. A vast extent of moor is visible, our range of vision being bounded by the distant heights of North Hisworthy, Great Mis Tor, Cut Hill, White Ridge, and Hameldon. But we are at the turf-tie, and something other than looking upon the scenery demands our attention.

Each farmer has his own particular tie, and it is an unwritten law, and one that is always respected, that none may interfere with it. It takes the form of a rectangular pit, usually about three or four feet in depth, its size depending upon the time its owner has been cutting peat from it. It is no uncommon thing for a farmer to keep himself supplied from one tie for twenty years, or even longer; there is, in fact, no necessity for him to open a new one except in the case of the peat deteriorating, or when he gets too near to the tie of his neighbour. Very often the peat is of great depth, and the further it is from the surface the better is its quality. But the Dartmoor man never goes too deep. By so doing he would not only give himself unnecessary trouble in throwing out the peat, but would also form dangerous pits.

When a new tie has to be opened, a narrow trench, forty yards in length and two or three feet deep, is first made, the work being similar to that of cutting a gutter or drain. The peat is then cut from the side of this trench as required, and thus the rectangular pit is gradually formed. The tie to which our companion has brought us is one that has been in use for some time, and we shall therefore be the better able to see how the work of procuring peat is performed.

It is the first cutting that has been made for the year, and the side of the tie will therefore require to be 'shaved'. This operation is performed with the long knife, an instrument consisting of a blade about two and a half feet in length and three or four inches in breadth, not unlike that of a straightened scythe, affixed to a handle of wood. When this is completed a cut is made in the ground parallel to the edge of the tie, and fourteen inches from it, with the same instrument. The depth of this cut entirely depends upon the nature of the 'heading', that is the soil filled with the roots of the heather. This is sometimes so thin that the peat comes to within a few inches of the surface, and at others it is two feet or more in thickness. If the ground round our tie had chanced to be of the former character our labourer, after making the cut, would have been able to remove the surface turf with an ordinary shovel. But it is not; the heading is very deep, and so he has to use the budding iron.

This may be likened to a flat, triangular-shaped shovel, with a straight handle. The labourer, getting into the tie, thrusts this into its side at the junction of the heading with the peat, keeping the face of the tool parallel to the surface of the ground. This he continues to do, working his way along the tie, and thrusting the budding-iron each time sufficiently far into the side of the tie to reach the perpendicular cut previously made with the knife. Lengths of about a couple of feet of this heading are cut off as he proceeds, and thrown into the tie, the green side being kept upward according to a recognised rule. It will be seen that when this operation is completed the peat is laid bare to a width of fourteen inches from one end of the tie to the other, and it is now ready for cutting.

The turf-iron is then brought into requisition. This is semi-circular in shape, one of the horns being turned up at right-angles, and is about seven inches wide. A flat socket of iron receives the wooden handle, in which is a 'shoulder', where the foot may be placed when an extra pressure is required to drive the tool into the peat. Standing on the uncovered strip at one end of the tie, with his face turned from it, and having it on his left hand, our companion, holding his iron at right angles to the edge, presses it into the peat, and brings away a small portion. This is repeated, the cutter moving backward, until he has got to the required depth of twenty inches. Again he thrusts it downward, not quite perpendicularly, and with a motion somewhat similar to that made in turning up ground with a spade, lifts out a slab of peat twenty inches long, seven inches wide, and two inches thick. The turned up end of his semi-circular blade really enables the cutter to make two cuts at right angles to each other at once, one being the width and the other the thickness of the slab. Our companion throws his first turf into the tie, and then cuts another from the inner half of his fourteen-inch strip, which is thrown on the ground on his right. This operation the labourer continues, half the slabs that he cuts going into the tie in rows three or four deep, and the other half being similarly disposed on the heather. They are of the average thickness of two inches, but in this the cutter has only his eye to guide him. When the forty yards forming the length of the tie have been gone over in this way our companion has completed a journey. No less than 1,440 slabs of peat have been cut, which cannot be called a bad half-day's work.

At the works at Rattle Brook Head, a different size slab from the ordinary was cut. Instead of being seven inches by two, they were four inches by four, and the journey consisted of sixty yards, the cutter's pay being arranged accordingly. The usual price paid is half a crown a journey.

When the peat is cut it has to be dried before it can be taken away. At first the slabs are stood up in pairs, one leaning against the other, and if the weather should remain hot and dry, and the

farmer be at leisure, it is possible to remove them in about two or
three weeks. But more often they have to be left for a longer
period, and are then formed into small piles called stooks, or if
necessary that they should remain until harvest is over, into larger
ones known as ricks. If there should be a long continuance of wet
weather, and the peat cannot be dried and brought away from
the ties, it becomes useless. When it is piled in the farmer's yard
the stacks are always thatched.

The situation of some ties renders it impossible to approach
them with a cart, and in those cases a turf barrow is employed.
This is furnished with a broad wheel in order that it may not sink
too deeply into the soft ground. The front part of the barrow is
very wide, and a large number of slabs of peat can be carried
in it. A journey will make a good cartload, and from thirty to
forty loads are required to supply a farmhouse for a year.

Among the most noted of former Dartmoor peat cutters may
be named Daniel Leaman, of Dartmeet, and Will Mann, of
Hexworthy. Today Daniel Leaman is represented by his son
William, and another who finds much work with the irons is
Coaker, of Swincombe. On the west side of the moor one who has
certainly done a full share of peat cutting is Richard Cudlipp, of
Mary Tavy, who worked many years ago in the tie at Rattle
Brook Head, and more lately on the hill at Skir.

Those who dwell on the borders of the moor have a long
distance to go for peat, since it can only be obtained in its more
central parts. Cottagers who have no means of fetching it have
therefore recourse to the practice of paring the surface turf, and
drying it, the slabs being known in this case as 'vags'. It is rather
amusing to find in a certain guide-book this word given as 'bags'.
B and V are sometimes interchangeable, it is true, but that they
should be so here is new to us. The change is, however, not without its use; it shows that the 'guide' was ignorant of one of the
commonest words heard on Dartmoor. The cutting of 'vags' has
wrought much injury to the pasturage in some places. On Black
Down, in Mary Tavy, where there is little depth of soil, the

practice was formerly carried on to such an extent as to almost denude many parts of it. At one time a vag-iron was used for cutting these slabs. It was in shape like a budding-knife, but was furnished with a 'wing', and was so large as to require two to work it, one pushing and the other drawing, in the same manner as 'spading' was sometimes done. Now, however, vag cutting is generally performed with an ordinary shovel.

The peat cutter has certainly left his mark upon the moor. Nowhere, except in the worst parts of the fen in the north quarter, is the ground so broken, and difficult to be passed over, as where he has been. He found Dartmoor rough, and he has contrived to make it a little rougher. Those who know what it is to find themselves in the midst of a network of turf ties on a dark night will not be disposed to dispute this.

The Dartmoor man instead of opening a new tie will often prefer to cut in a very old disused one. The peat is always good there, he will tell you, 'vur the old men knawed what they was about as well as us do'.

THE WARRENER

THE present signification of the word warren is not quite the same as once it was. In early times it meant a privileged place, and along with the wild beasts of the forest and the chase, the beasts and fowls of the warren were protected by the King 'for his princely delight and pleasure'. The latter were the hare and coney, the pheasant and the partridge. Now a warren is a tract of land, enclosed or otherwise, set apart for the keeping of rabbits, and in this form there is evidence that they have existed on Dartmoor for a considerable period. None, however, can be adduced from place-names, unless Conies Down, near the head of the Cowsic, be a possible exception. But whether this name has reference to rabbits, or is a corruption of an older one to which no such connection belongs, is not certain. There can be little doubt that the place is the same as that mentioned in a document of the time of Edward III as Condyshull. It occurs in an account of John D'Abernon, constable of Lydford Castle, and is set down as being in the west quarter of the Forest, where the present Conies Down is situated. Other evidence that the places are identical is afforded by the fact that the pasturage on this down is good, and it is as a grazing ground that it is mentioned in the account. Another name that would seem to point to the early existence of a warren on the moor occurs on North Bovey Common, where a rock-pile eastward of the Moreton road is sometimes called Warren Tor. But its true name is Birch Tor, and the former cannot be shown to be any other than a modern appellation. New Warren Tor on the Plym is also a name of recent date, the rocks so called being properly a part of Leggis Tor.

The most important warrens on the moor are Ditsworthy, Hen Tor, and Trowlsworthy, in the valley of the Plym; and Headland, New House, and Soussons, near the sources of the Walla Brook and the West Webburn. Others are Huntingdon, on the Avon, at the southern end of the Forest; a small one at Skaigh, on the northern slope of Cosdon; and also at Shipley, on the verge of Brent Moor. A few years ago a warren was formed in Longaford newtake, on the West Dart above Two Bridges, in which enclosure is situated the well-known Wistman's Wood. In Gidleigh Chase there was anciently one, and a warren also formerly existed on the side of Mis Tor, and another on Dartmeet Hill.

Ditsworthy warren is situated in the parish of Sheepstor, and is of considerable extent, being the largest warren on Dartmoor. It is in the occupation of Mrs Ware, in which family it has been for a long period. In addition to this warren Mrs Ware also holds the adjoining one of Leggis Tor, usually called New warren; Hen Tor warren, in the parish of Shaugh, on the other side of the Plym; and a portion of the Forest near the headwaters of that river. This immense tract of ground covers an area of several square miles, its boundaries including some of the most solitary, as well as the most interesting, parts of south-western Dartmoor.

The warren house is situated on the southern slope of Eastern Tor, which crowns a low eminence mostly covered with short turf. No other habitation is near, and save for a glimpse of the distant Cornish hills with the Channel beyond, nothing but the moor is seen. With the exception of a single ash, bearing unmistakable signs of the buffetings it has received from the winter storms, there are no trees around this solitary dwelling, which is sheltered only by the rising ground behind it, and towards the west. A few enclosures adjoin, and a rough track leads down to the river, where there is a ford, and a clam, or wooden footbridge, high above the water.

But though far removed from the cultivated country, the approach to Ditsworthy warren house is not difficult. On the side of the hill to the west a short piece of road leads to Ringmoor Down, over which, although there is no regular track, a wheeled conveyance may readily pass. Its surface is remarkably even, and no common in the Dartmoor country is more free from furze and heather. The way is marked by small heaps of stones placed at short distances apart, which, although not necessary in fine weather when distant landmarks are visible, are useful enough in a mist. A Plymothian assisted in the work of collecting and piling up these stones. This was Mr George Davis, at one time the land-lord of the Old Four Castles Inn, that formerly stood in Old Town Street. Mr Davis met with an accident, which resulted in a broken leg, and when convalescent went to Ditsworthy on a visit. It was during the time he was there that the work was carried out, and he put the finishing touches to it by giving the stones a coat of whitewash. This, however, the Dartmoor rains have long since removed.

There is another way by which a cart may reach Ditsworthy. This is by a track running northward from the houses, and joining the rough mine road that comes in from beyond Eylesbarrow, which is formed for some distance on the line of the old Abbots' Way. It leads to Meavy, passing Ringmoor Cot, close to which the path across the down joins it, and a branch also runs to Sheepstor.

Trowlsworthy warren adjoins Hen Tor, the two being separated by an affluent of the Plym named Spanish Lake, which little stream acts as the northern boundary of the warren. Its western boundary is the Plym, and its southern the Blackabrook, the eastern being formed by a line drawn from the latter stream to Spanish Lake. This tract of land, which is probably not much less than a thousand acres in extent, lies within the parish of Shaugh, and is said to have been a warren from very early times. In the middle of the sixteenth century it was conveyed to William Woollcombe, and in that family it still remains.

The warren house stands on the side of a hill above the Plym, and is in full view from Cadaford Bridge. The approach is by a road branching from that leading to Lee Moor and Cornwood, and which is carried over the Blackabrook by a clapper bridge. Adjoining the house are several enclosures, and the soil and situation being not altogether unfriendly, a little corn is usually

The Warrener The cabin of the warrener at Wistman's warren. Crow Tor on the skyline, right. All trace of the cabin has disappeared but a small emplacement and a few low ruined walls can be found at the north end of the wood. From the frontispiece of *The River*, first edition, 1902, by Eden Phillpotts

The Warrener Mrs Ware, the warrener at Ditsworthy, in her kitchen sometime between the wars

The Miner   Water-wheel at White Works. None of these remain on Dartmoor.
Photograph by Robert Burnard, 1 June 1889

The Miner   Henroost Mine, near Hexworthy, about 1914. A few ruined walls
are all that may be seen there now

grown. Higher up the hill are the two tors of Great and Little Trowlsworthy.

The present occupant of Trowlsworthy warren is Richard Lavers—not Davis, as he is referred to in a certain book, the writer of which once called upon him to inquire the way to a group of antiquities on the hill. He is eighty-four years of age, hale and hearty, and able to take his share of work. With his fine open face, mild blue eyes, and skin as hard, brown, and shiny as a saddle, he is the true type of a Dartmoor man, and no better specimen of one will be found between Yes Tor and the Western Beacon. In his calling of warrener he follows the vocation of his father, and amid the same burrows, for he, too, lived at Trowlsworthy. He has had nine sons, of whom four are living, born to him, and one daughter. His son Thomas lives with him at the warren, and the best we can wish him is that he will prove to be as good a man and live so long as his father.

Richard Lavers' earlier days were not passed on the warren, but he has spent sixty-three years upon it. It is a lonely life, he says, and if he had his day to go over again he would not choose it. Yet there are some who love to dwell amid the solitude of the moor. We have known those who have grown old on the waste, and who, looking back over their long lives, could truly say they had never had any other wish but to remain there. At the present time Robert Phillips, a young man, is employed on the warren at Ditsworthy, and he prefers to work, he says, on the lonely moor rather than in the in-country.

The entrance to Trowlsworthy warren house is reached through a small courtyard, enclosed by a very high wall. When I was quite a child I remember hearing how a fox was once captured here. He was in the habit of making free with the poultry occasionally, probably desiring a change from rabbits. One Sunday morning, during the absence of the inmates, he contrived to scale the wall of this courtyard, attracted possibly by the sight of some chickens which had been left there, and which he was able to view through the barred gate. The consequence may be imagined, and so also may the feelings with which Reynard's work was viewed. Warreners are good trappers, and though a fox may be a bit sharper than a rabbit, he did not prove to be a match for the wit of Trowlsworthy. On the following Sunday morning something was placed against the wall of the yard on the outside, and something was taken away from the inside. Then one or two chickens —certainly not the best of the brood—were put in the yard, and the trap was ready. Reynard entered it. He climbed the wall, and with the aid of what had been put against it made his way down a board that acted as a sort of shute. But it had no bearing as on the previous Sunday, and as soon as he was fairly on it it fell into the yard, carrying the robber with it. There was no escape, and Reynard paid the penalty of his crimes. This was in the days, be it understood, when no subsidy was received from the hunt.

Huntingdon warren was formed by John Michelmore in the beginning of the nineteenth century, and included an earlier holding. In a certificate of the date 1759, setting forth some tin bounds, there is mention of Huntingdon East Gate, and it is said that a house and newtake existed there before 1700. In 1809 John Michelmore obtained a ninety-nine years' lease of the place from the Duchy, on undertaking to enclose 600 acres and create a warren. In 1882 William Michelmore, who had inherited the property, sold the residue of the lease to Mr E. Fearnley Tanner, who bought it to protect the foxes, as he was then hunting a part of the country with his own pack of foxhounds. On giving up hounds in 1887 Mr Tanner let the warren, Mr Fortescue, Mr Broad, and Mr Harris being tenants in succession. It is now let by Mr Tanner at a low rental to the Dartmoor Hunt for the protection of foxes.

The warren house at Huntingdon, like that at Ditsworthy, stands apart from any other. Nothing but the moor is in sight, but the in-country becomes visible on ascending the slope behind the dwelling. At one time Huntingdon was a flourishing warren, the nature of the ground over which the greater part of it extends being well suited to the purpose.

Soussons warren extends northward from the road leading from Post Bridge to Widecombe. It belongs to Mr Eives, and is now occupied by Messrs Leaman and Widecombe. The name of Hannaford will still be found at Headland, although the older occupier passed away a few years ago. New House warren is, perhaps, better known than any on Dartmoor, lying as it does close to the Moreton highway. The warren house is also a hostelry, and though with scarce a 'neighbour roof', it is certain that its inmates do not find company entirely lacking. Hext, the warrener, bears a name that has been known on Dartmoor for centuries. These three warrens, which are close to each other, are large, probably averaging not less than a thousand acres each.

Wistman's Wood warren, so familiar to the readers of Eden Phillpotts' delightful Dartmoor story, *The River*, was formed about nine years ago by Mr Jones Saltoun, and is about 330 acres in extent. When the reader is introduced to the warrener, Nicholas Edgecombe, he finds him spinning rabbit snares from copper wire. Such are always used at Wistman's warren, but in the other larger ones the greater number of the rabbits are caught in nets. The wire snares are usually placed on the little creeps, tiny paths, which, if you carefully observe the ground around the burrows, you will see running in various directions. But some warreners will not use them, preferring to catch all their rabbits in the nets. These are usually 300 feet long, and 20 meshes, or about 5 feet, in width, and are hung upon upright sticks placed a few yards apart, the upper cord of the net being about two and a half feet from the ground. Sometimes they are placed round a burrow, and at others stretched in a long line of fifteen or twenty nets across a piece of ground. In the former case ferrets are employed. These are put in the burrow, and as the rabbits are bolted they entangle themselves in the meshes of the net. In the latter case the mode of proceeding is altogether different. Let the warrener show us how he goes to work.

It is a cheerless evening, and as you leave the warren house and feel the cold breath of air that sweeps down from the naked hills, you think what a pity it is they do not catch rabbits in the summer and during the day-time. But the warrener takes no notice of it. Carrying a huge bundle of nets he plods onward, followed by his assistant, who is laden in a similar manner. By-and-by you reach the beginning of a row of sticks, which have been stuck into the ground during the day, and the work of hanging up the nets commences. On one side of the row are some burrows, on the other are the rabbits. They have left their snug habitations to feed in quietness at night, and the warrener's first work is to take care that they shall not get back again.

The nets being hung the warrener returns to the house, which you do not feel particularly sorry for. When he calls you very early on the following morning you cannot help regretting that you have been so rash as to express a desire to go with him. But it is too late to retreat, and you rise and dress to the accompaniment of chattering teeth. Once more you make your way towards where the rabbits are feeding, and getting behind them drive them into the nets, being assisted in your work by spaniels. The warrener seizes the rabbits as they vainly endeavour to pass the nets, and kills them instantly by twisting their necks. When you look upon the heap of slain you are astonished.

The burrows, or burys, as the warrener calls them, are formed by first digging a narrow trench, with small ones branching from it on each side, but not opposite to each other. Large slabs of turf are then cut, and with these the little trenches are covered. Over this is heaped a mound of earth, and the burrow is finished. A few holes are made for the rabbits to enter, and they quickly take possession of their new abode.

During hard winters, when food is scarce, the rabbits have to be fed, or they will leave the warren. This is a part of the warrener's work that has to be carefully attended to. Any neglect may result in considerable loss. The rabbits are usually fed on furze and hay.

The trapping season usually commences at the end of August or beginning of September, and lasts until the end of February or beginning of March. The warrens in the Plym valley find a market for their rabbits in Plymouth and Devonport, though from Ditsworthy many are sent to Birmingham. Birmingham and Sheffield are also markets for those caught in the warrens on the east side of the moor, the rabbits being dispatched from Moreton-hampstead.

But the warrener's profits are declining. There are no such times now as those when the skin-packing at Ditsworthy was as important a matter as the wool-packing of an in-country farmer—when as much as £110 was received for skins in one year. Now that is over; the rabbits have to be sold in their skins, and much that once belonged to the warrener is lost to him. Prices are lower, too, than they were. Farmers take a great many rabbits to market now, and the warrener feels the competition. But what he has chiefly suffered from during late years is the scarcity of rabbits on the moor. In the great blizzard of 1891 thousands of rabbits died on Dartmoor, and the effect of the partial depopulation of the warrens in that year is still felt.

THE MINER

PROBABLY at no period of its history has mining altogether ceased on Dartmoor, though comparatively little has been done in that direction during recent times. Of the several mines enumerated in Moore's *History of Devonshire* as being worked on the moor in the early years of the nineteenth century, all but Vitifer are now idle, and that until about twelve months ago had been closed for thirty years. Another is now also working near Hexworthy, and these two represent the Dartmoor mining at present. There are a few mines to be found on the borders of the moor, but none besides these on the common lands.

Hexworthy Mine, as it is usually called, was opened about fourteen years ago on the site of some old workings. These were mostly situated in a valley known as Skir Gert, through which runs the Wobrook, an affluent of the West Dart. The little stream rises on the high land of the south quarter of the Forest, not very far from Aune Head, but takes an opposite course to that river. Flowing northward for nearly a mile, it turns abruptly towards the east, and enters the valley named, which is formed by Skir Hill on one side and Down Ridge on the other. Though this valley is always spoken of as a gert, the latter term is more often applied to the deep trenches excavated by the miners, and seen in many parts of the moor, than to natural hollows or passes. Near the foot of an ancient working called Dry Lakes the Wobrook leaves the gert, and, making a bend, again flows northward, forming in this latter part of its course the boundary between the Forest and Holne Moor. This valley was long ago streamed for tin. Old workings are numerous, and to one of them there is incidental reference in an early document, being a copy of another of thirteenth century date. Evidences that it was also the scene of the tinners' operations in a later time, but yet in a day far

64

removed from the present, have also been forthcoming. When the modern mine was started, an old shaft was discovered in a deep working known as Henroost, not far from the source of the Wobrook, and on Down Ridge there was an ancient adit. We, therefore, know that the tin-seeker laboured here in an early day, and also in medieval times.

The name of the working just referred to seems to point to a time prior to that when it was customary to sink shafts, and if this is really so the latter must have been sunk on the site of still older operations. When we first knew Henroost, about five and thirty years ago, there was a story current in the locality connecting it with the familiar bird of the farmyard, evidently invented, as in so many similar cases, to account for the name, which there is no doubt is a corruption of Celtic words. There is another name further down the valley about which the same may be said. This is Hooten Wheals, a gully covered with the debris of the tinner, and which it has been suggested is a corruption of Wooden Wheels, and to have reference to the water-wheels of the miners. This is not an impossible derivation, since in the Devon vernacular 'wooden' would become 'ooden', but it is not a very likely one. There is no need to suppose that 'wheals' in this connection ever meant anything other than what is now understood by the word in the West Country—a tin or copper mine. We could never find anyone who had heard of wheels having been seen at the spot in question. The late Mr Richard Cleave, of Hexworthy, told us many years ago that there certainly had been none there in his time, and he had never heard his father, whose recollection went back to the latter part of the eighteenth century, speak of any.

The modern operations on the site of these old workings at Skir were, after a few years, suspended for a short time. They are now, however, being conducted with increased energy, and it is stated that the prospects of the mine are good. About thirty men are at present employed, most of them coming from a distance, and these live at the mine during the week. Many of them belong to the Buckfastleigh district, and until recently several came from

E

Mary Tavy, journeying over the moor by way of Princetown. Others live at White Works and at Hexworthy.

From Princetown the Mary Tavy men followed the route across Tor Royal newtake to Swincombe, where there is a ford over the stream of that name, and also stepping-stones. But during a heavy flood it was not possible to cross by means of the latter, and a wooden footbridge was therefore erected. This proved of great service, and in part realised the wishes of old John Bishop, who lived close by, and who seemed to think that when it was possible to drive over the Swincombe at this point, instead of through it, there would be nothing else wanted on Dartmoor.

Vitifer Mine is situated at the head of the West Webburn, on the common belonging to the parish of North Bovey. It is about half a mile outside the boundary of the Forest, and two and a half miles from Post Bridge. Lysons in the volume of the *Magna Britannia* containing the account of Devon, speaks of Vitifer as about to be abandoned in 1820. The mine was upon a large scale, he says, and had been productive. Somewhere about that time it appears to have been worked by a Mr Paul who is said to have made a considerable amount of money there. Like Hexworthy Mine, it is on the site of ancient workings. An old circular shaft, 15 fathoms deep, and lined with stone in the manner of a well, was found about the time Mr Paul was in possession of the mine, and this was deepened and worked. The hollow in which it was discovered is still known as Wall Shaft Gully.

Water is brought to Vitifer from the East Dart by means of a leat, which the name of a certain hill close to the intake in all probability shows to have been in existence for a long period. This is Lade Hill, and along its side the watercourse is conducted for some distance. Lade signifies a ditch or drain, or a cut which 'leads' water, from the Anglo-Saxon 'lad', a canal, or conduit, and is indeed only another form of 'leat'. We can, therefore, hardly come to any other conclusion than that the hill took its name from the watercourse, and if this is so it would go to prove that the latter has some claim to antiquity. The intake, which is at a spot on the river called Sandy Hole, is exactly $3\frac{1}{2}$ miles in a straight line from the mine, but the leat is carried over more than double that distance, being skilfully conducted around the hills.

Vitifer Mine does not appear to have proved very successful during the times it was worked subsequent to its relinquishment by Mr Paul, and soon after 1870 it was abandoned. But the sett is nevertheless considered to be a valuable one, and with modern dressing machinery the adventurers who have recently restarted the mine—Mr W. R. Phelips, of Montacute, in Somerset, and Mr W. A. Padfield, of Exeter—consider there is every reason to hope for satisfactory results. About twelve months ago work was commenced at the mine, and during that time much has been done. Two water-wheels have been fixed, tramroads have been laid down and a shaft has been sunk to a depth of about seven fathoms. Already something has been accomplished in the direction of stamping the ore thrown away in former days, and it has yielded a good percentage of tin. Mr Webb is the captain of the mine, and he anticipates a success for it when it is properly developed. About twenty men are at present employed, and these live at and around Post Bridge, and at King's Oven, near New House. As the work progresses more will, of course, be needed, so that there is a probability that ere long Vitifer, for so many years deserted by the miner, will once more become a busy scene of labour.

About two years since a mine was started near Mary Tavy, but in Peter Tavy parish. It is, however, not on the moor, though only a short distance from its border. It is known as the Devon United Mines, and, like the others we have named, is on the site of a former venture, the old working having borne the name of Wheal Anne. Mr Bowhay is the captain, and he is confident that the mine is rich. Although operations have not long been in progress many tons of tin have been raised and sold, and better things are expected when the 'old men's' workings are reached.

At this mine the men are paid by the day. The underground

men, that is the miners proper, and the labourers who are employed with them, work in three cores, or shifts, of eight hours each, one going on at six in the morning, the second at two in the afternoon, and the third at ten at night. The hours of work of the stamp men and the furnace men are different. About thirty-five men are employed, who live for the most part in the immediate neighbourhood, but a few come from Tavistock. At Hexworthy Mine the men are on what is known as tut work; that is, they are paid a certain sum per fathom of ground excavated.

Of all the places around Dartmoor, Mary Tavy is the only one that can be said to have had any real importance as a mining parish in modern times. But the mines to which it owed its reputation are now closed. Wheal Friendship and Wheal Betsy, once very large concerns, gradually dwindled down to nothing; the latter has been for a long time abandoned, and two years ago the former ceased working. Mary Tavy has, however, always been a home of the miner, and has furnished many men for the mines of South and West Africa and India.

Closer to the moor even than the Devon United Mines is the copper mine at Ramsleigh, near South Zeal, but like the former it can scarcely be regarded as a Dartmoor mine proper. Nor can those at Christow on the Teign, for although it is probable that the commons around that place were once joined to the main portion of the moor, cultivation has long since cut them off from it.

Not a few old paths on Dartmoor are the work of the miner, and several have been made by him in recent times. The clapper at Knock Mine on the Taw owes its existence to him, and so in all probability does the clapper known as New Bridge on the Black-a-ven, a tributary of the East Ockment. New Bridge consists of a centre pier and buttresses, and is in a good state of preservation. Knock Mine Bridge, or, as it is sometimes called, Steeperton Bridge, from its proximity to the tor of that name, is not so interesting. It is 29 feet long and 15 feet wide, and there are four openings. Several of the blocks that formed the roadway have been displaced.

A path over White Ridge was marked out by a miner who worked at Knock Mine. He lived at Stannon, near Post Bridge, and his way to the scene of his labour lay over the ridge to the circles known as the Grey Wethers, thence through the enclosures of Teign Head, and over the side of Newtake to the Steeperton Brook and the Taw—a wild and solitary walk. A road runs out to the mine from Belstone, one small portion of it being paved with flat stones.

Whether the expectations that have been formed respecting Dartmoor mining will be fulfilled remains to be seen. At present the industry, not only on the moor, but throughout the country, is the opposite of flourishing. Since the early years of the nineteenth century, when mining was certainly in a bad state, it has witnessed some improvement, but only to fall back into its former condition. According to Lysons, the average quantity of tin that Devonshire produced in the six years preceding Michaelmas, 1820, was just under thirty tons, at which time there were several mines at work on Dartmoor, Vitifer, Eylesbarrow, and White Works being among the number. In 1893 fifty-two tons were raised in the county, thirty tons of this being produced by the Hexworthy Mine.

Today no more than about fifty men are employed on Dartmoor in the search for tin, and as many of these have their homes outside its borders it cannot be said that it forms a large share of the work of the native. Probably he prefers gathering cattle or cutting peat under a blue sky—or even a grey one—to burrowing in the earth like a rabbit, and if so he has only the instincts of the 'old men'. In every valley on the moor are the workings of the latter found, and except in a few, and those probably of comparatively modern date, there has been no attempt to go beneath the surface. They were content to work there, obtaining their tin by the process known as streaming, and it is not unlikely that they found it sufficiently profitable. But they left nothing there for their brothers of today; they have to penetrate into the bowels of the earth to obtain their reward.

THE QUARRYMAN

THOUGH granite in small quantities has always been obtained from Dartmoor, as old buildings in its neighbourhood amply testify, it was not until the opening of the quarries at Hey Tor, in the parish of Ilsington, and those on Walkhampton Common, not far from Princetown, a little over eighty years ago, that it became an article of commerce. Operations at the former quarries ceased long since, and at the latter they have not been continuous. These, however, have now been working for several years, and others have been started in their vicinity. Granite was obtained from Walkhampton Common prior to 1808, for the purposes of the war prison and barracks at Princetown, and it is not unlikely that this led to the possibility of profitably quarrying it there being considered. With the completion of the horse tramroad from Plymouth to Princetown in 1823, the deportation of large quantities of granite from this part of the moor commenced. An important industry sprang up, and though there came a period when the sound of the workman's tool was unheard, it once more flourished, and was further developed, when the present railway took the place of the older road.

A description of these quarries in 1831 is preserved in the diary of the Rev E. A. Bray, the vicar of Tavistock, who visited them in the month of May in that year. His object was not, however, to see them, but to trace the railroad to Princetown, and as this led him by the workings he noted what he saw. This did not please him; he laments the destruction of the tors, and frankly confesses that he was in a humour to give the workmen more blame than praise for their industry. He peevishly refers to the manager, or someone then in charge of the quarries, as 'Mr Johnson, or Thompson, or a person of some such name', and when he was informed by a man who accosted him that he might see the works

if he wished, tells us that he 'was not so desirous of seeing what
had been done as what had been left undone.' We are as much
opposed to the destruction of the rock towers that add such an
interest to the moor as ever Mr Bray was, but it would be useless
to lose one's temper about it. At the present time we are glad to
find that, for the most part, it is not considered necessary to do
such damage as he deplored.

Mr Bray reached the railroad near Walkhampton, which, he
says, reminded him of a garden walk with an iron edging in place
of a box one. He is not quite certain of the names of the tors on
the right of the railroad, so he mentions them numerically. The
first one he reached appeared to have been abandoned by the
workmen for some time, but much destruction had been wrought
there. Below it were lying squared masses of granite, and others
which he says caused him to think of the teeth of the mammoth.
These were such as may be seen anywhere on the edge of the
moor. They were blocks that had been split by means of wedges,
and, as Mr Bray observes, their serrated appearance was due to
the holes made in them to receive these.

The mode of splitting stones now practised is the same as was
adopted then, and is called by the workmen 'feather and tear'.
Holes about three inches in depth, or more if necessary, and from
five to six inches apart, are drilled in the block required to be
split, and into these are inserted wedges, two pieces of thin iron
—usually hoop-iron—having previously been placed in each.
Between these pieces the wedges are driven, and then successively
struck until the stone is split.

At the second tor reached by Mr Bray a number of men were
at work, so many that he says it might almost be compared to an
ant-hill. One of them, who was standing on a very large stone,
picking it into shape with 'a pickaxe as ponderous as a sledge-
hammer', he likens to a statue put in action. The drapery may
not have been so well disposed as in some scenic groups, he says,
but the muscular development was far better. Near this tor were
some huts and a blacksmith's shop, and on the tramway a rude

carriage with an awning. Conveyances of this kind were used, he supposes, by pleasure parties who made excursions from Plymouth, and he suggests that they were probably as 'uneasy as the scythed cars of the Britons'. What the latter may have been like can, of course, only be imagined, but Mr Bray was quite wrong in thinking that there was any discomfort attached to riding on the tram-wagons. I have ridden on them frequently, both when laden with granite, or when returning to the quarries empty, and, cumbrous though they were, they ran smoothly enough. Mr Bray here ascended an inclined plane of great breadth, on which were chains running upon rollers, and this brought him to a quarry where men were engaged in loading the wagons, two immense cranes being employed for the purpose. The centre of the tor had been laid open, and its summit towered perhaps sixty or seventy feet above them. 'Every recourse had been had to artificial as well as natural powers in this work of destruction.'

A considerable opening had also been made in the third tor that Mr Bray passed, but here there was no inclined plane, the granite being drawn from the quarry by horses. On reaching the fourth tor, which he supposed to be King Tor, he saw a number of men working on detached rocks, thrown about in picturesque confusion, but which he was convinced they would soon reduce to a heap of rubbish. Here his examination of the quarries, or rather of the tramway, terminated for that day, but he returned a week later and resumed it.

Reaching that part of the railroad above the curve at King Tor, where it doubled back upon itself, as does the present Princetown railway, which, in this part of its course is formed almost on the same line, he followed it for a short distance, and then leaving it made his way over the neck of land it partly encircled. This, of course, brought him to the tors he had visited in the previous week, though he expresses surprise at finding such was the case. By this, however, he learnt something. He discovered that the workmen did not hesitate to vary or change the names of the tors as suited them, for the Swill Tor of a few days before had now become Swell Tor, and the rock pile above the quarry he was informed was Inclined Plane Tor! He does not seem to have pushed his inquiries in this direction any farther, but contents himself with remarking that in his researches on the moor he could seldom meet with two persons who gave the same names to the tors.

Returning to the tramway, he reached the branch known as Royal Oak siding, though he does not call it by that name. Here there was a long shed, from which came the sounds of stonecutters at work on the stones obtained in the quarry to which the siding led. Some immense columns were lying near, which one of the workmen told him were intended for a market about to be built in London; and further on he saw parts of others. From this point Mr Bray made his way by the tramway to the prison, and thence returned to Tavistock.

One cannot but agree with him that the destruction of what he terms the hallowed vestiges of a former world should have been avoided, but it is impossible to do so when he suggests an alternative to open quarrying. The latter there must be, much as we may lament the disfiguration of the landscape in consequence. If the tors and objects of antiquarian interest are spared, we cannot very well expect more. Mr Bray's plan of obtaining granite was by quarrying underground, and thus, by forming catacombs, add to, instead of diminishing, the interest of the locality. These would afford occasional shelter from the storms, he says, and might enable the men to work at all seasons. 'Who knows', he asks, 'but in time the catacombs of Dartmoor may be as famous as those of Egypt?' And who knows, we would ask, what we shall hear next? We venture to think that Mr Bray was much nearer to his true avocation when fulfilling his duties as vicar of Tavistock, than when offering suggestions on granite quarrying.

The first of the Walkhampton Common quarries to be opened appear to have been those nearest Princetown, one of which was at the point known as the Royal Oak and the other a short distance from it, the latter being called the Higher Quarry. Close by was a row of dwellings, and these, although the walls have been coated with tar as a protection from the weather, still bear the name of the Red Cottages. These accommodated many who were employed on the works, but a number lived elsewhere, a few of them at Rundle Stone, about a mile distant, where were some of the rudest huts to be seen on the moor. A small place of worship, the Foggin Tor, or as it was more often called, the Royal Oak chapel, was erected near the cottages. Work at Swell Tor must, however, have commenced shortly after the opening of the tramway, or such progress as Mr Bray speaks of could not have been made by 1831.

The tramway and the quarries were in the hands of one company, and the former continued in regular use until 1865, granite being daily dispatched to the Cattewater. In that year the line was acquired by another company, who held it until about 1879, when that portion of it extending from the eastern verge of Roborough Down to its termination at Princetown, was purchased by the Princetown Railway Co, who constructed their line upon it throughout the greater part of its course. Sidings were formed at the quarries, and the granite has since been conveyed over it.

The Swell Tor quarries only are now worked, the higher ones being disused. They are held under lease from Sir Massey Lopes by Messrs Pethick, of Plymouth, and about ninety men are at present employed, though during the past summer there have been more than this. Some of these live at Princetown and Rundle Stone, and others come from a greater distance. The manager of the works is Mr George Mitchell, an American.

About thirty years ago a quarry was opened near Merivale Bridge, on the common belonging to the parish of Whitchurch. It was worked by the late Mr William Duke, who had previously had the management of the Royal Oak Quarry, and is now in the hands of Messrs C. L. Duke and Co. The works are known as the Tor Quarries, and during the past few years great development has been witnessed. The granite is said to be of a particularly fine quality, and for certain kinds of work is much in demand.

The Clay Labourer Old photographs of the clay works are very scarce. These show labourers at work at Redlake after the period covered by this book, but depict the methods used in Crossing's time. The men are Waye and Warren, and the horse was called Violet. Photographs by Mr J. Spencer

The Sportsman Part of the crowd assembled on Bellaford Day to see the meet at Bellaford Tor—early in the century

The stone is put on the railway at Tavistock, over four miles distant. Horses were used for drawing it until about two years ago, when a traction engine was substituted.

Mr William Bolt is the manager of the Tor Quarries, and about 140 men are now employed; a few months ago, however, there were as many as 170. Some of these have been on the works ever since they were opened. Many now live on the spot, a number of cottages having recently been built there, and others come from Princetown, Horrabridge, Tavistock, and neighbouring villages. A Wesleyan chapel has also been opened, and from a place consisting of only a few cottages and a roadside inn, Merivale is fast becoming a village.

A quarry has also been opened during the past two or three years in the valley under Heckwood Tor, less than a mile from Merivale, and another at Lowery Stent, on the northern side of the Burrator Lake. At the latter several men are working who come from the neighbourhood of Kit Hill, on the Cornish side of the Tamar, and these mostly live at Dousland. Granite was obtained at Heckwood many years ago for the Plymouth breakwater. This was taken to Morwellham, and there put on board the barges that bore it to its destination.

Not far from Heckwood is Pu Tor, around which there has been quarrying on a small scale for a number of years. Much of the stone worked here, however, was surface granite, or what is termed 'grass rock'. Near Pu Tor is a pile of rocks sometimes called Sampford Tor; here the quarryman is busy, and to such an extent as to threaten the destruction of the whole cluster. There is also a quarry belonging to the prison at Princetown, and a disused quarry of red granite at Trowlsworthy. Granite was also formerly obtained in the valley near Good-a-Meavy, and quarries were opened on the southern verge of the moor during the time the works in connection with the South Devon Railway were in progress. One of these was at Woolholes, on Brent Moor, and another near Ivybridge. A considerable quantity of granite was also quarried on the slope below the Western Beacon several years ago, when the new viaducts at Ivybridge and Cornwood were built.

Mr Bray has spoken of the recourse made to artificial power in the work at the quarries. Could he visit Swell Tor or Merivale today he would find that this was so to a very much greater extent than in his time. What would he say to some of the monster blasts that now take place there? In March of last year an operation was conducted at Swell Tor by Mr W. H. Baron, the electrician, who like Mr Mitchell, the manager, is an American, by which many hundreds of tons of material were removed. Mr Baron having completed his preparations, all the employees withdrew out of danger. He then coolly inspected the wires and departed over the hill. There was a few minutes pause, and then a terrific roar awoke the echoes of the moor. As one bystander said, the hill appeared to move. One stone that was shifted by the discharge measured 23 feet long, and was 9 feet wide and 8 feet thick. In March of the present year a huge quantity of granite was also blasted at Merivale. Four holes were drilled to an average depth of 15 feet 3 inches, and were charged with 100 pounds of rock powder. These were then connected with an electric battery by means of a wire 200 yards long, and on the discharge taking place a mass of granite estimated to contain about 22,000 cubic feet, and to weigh 1,577 tons, was removed from its bed. The battery at Merivale is placed in a small erection of granite, roofed with thick slabs, on which is a layer of turf, and during the blasting operations a danger flag is hoisted on the hill near the quarry.

The tools used by the quarrymen are much the same as ever they were, and consist of jumper, the borer, stone picks, points, chisels, and the muckle, but he is greatly aided by the use of modern machinery. Steam derricks and steam travelling cranes are now used, and other appliances that enable him to perform his work more efficiently and easily.

The working of the stone after it has been quarried is a very important branch of the granite industry on the moor. Anything that can be fashioned out of granite is made there; channelling, kerbing, pitching, rollers, corbels, pillars, and even gravestones, with lettering complete. It is not improbable that Mr Bray would have felt some sort of gratification had they made the latter objects on the moor in his day, and had erected one on Swell Tor bearing an inscription to the effect that the granite industry on Dartmoor was defunct.

THE CLAY LABOURER

MUCH has been written lately about the china clay industry in Devon and Cornwall. It is stated that three-fourths of the works do not yield adequate profits, and with a view to amend this state of things the formation of a combine, or syndicate, of proprietors has been suggested. In the opinion of a Cornish manager of considerable experience, an association of producers having for its aim the obtaining of better prices would prove of benefit both to the employer and the workman, while the stability of the industry would remain uninjured. Several of the proprietors have been approached on the subject, but it is said that nothing has yet resulted. Overtures to the owners of clayworks have also been recently made on behalf of a proposed American combine, but were not received with favour. The china clay industry is a very important one, being essential to the potter, or manufacturer of china, the bleacher, and the paper-maker. Its transference would tend to cripple these, and it is, therefore, a matter for congratulation that no sympathy was extended to the proposal. There appears to be no reason why the industry should not be held. As the chief partner of the principal clay works in Devon has pointedly remarked, 'What is good enough for an American trust to try to buy is good enough for us to keep.'

In the china clay industry Dartmoor has a share, and it is quite possible that what has been said about the undertakings in the West Country generally may apply to some of the works to be found there, but this is a question that does not come within the scope of our remarks. We have to view the industry merely as one affording employment to a number of dwellers on the moor, or on its verge. It is not so much of the clay, which is the prepared product of decomposed granite, or of the mode of making it ready for the market, that we would speak, as of those who perform the labour attendant on its production, and the effect the industry has had upon that part of the moor in which the clay is procured.

As in the case of granite quarrying, the raising of clay is confined to a comparatively small area. The latter is found chiefly
near the headwaters of the Torry, an affluent of the Plym, rising
under Pen Beacon, and on the commons on each side of that
stream, the district over which works exist extending from Cadaford Bridge, on the Plym, to Crownhill Down and Headon Down,
near Cornwood. This is situated in the parishes of Cornwood,
Plympton St Mary, and Shaugh, while one pit is in the parish of
Meavy. Clay exists in other parts of Dartmoor, and has been
worked at Hey Tor and on Brent Moor.

The undertakings in the district lying round the upper Torry
belong to various proprietors. Messrs Watts, Blake, Bearne, & Co,
of Newton Abbot, have pits on Headon Down, and also near the
Plym. One of the latter is that alluded to as being in the parish of
Meavy, and is situated on the slope of Wigford Down, close to
the road leading from Cornwood to Dousland; the other is on the
opposite side of the river, below Saddlesborough, and is named
Shaugh Lake. From these pits the clay is washed down to the
works at Shaugh Bridge, whence it is carted to Bickleigh for
dispatch by rail. From the pits on Headon Down the clay is taken
to Cornwood station. There is also a clay works at Wotter, above
the valley of the Torry, and about a mile and a half south-east of
Shaugh. From these the clay is conveyed to Cornwood, a traction
engine being used for the purpose. From some of the pits on
Crownhill Down the clay is carted to Plympton.

But by far the most important undertaking in this neighbourhood, and indeed the largest of any kind on Dartmoor, is that of
Messrs Martin Brothers Limited at Lee Moor, where some of the
best quality clay in the West Country is produced. These works
were started in 1834 by the father of the late Mr John Phillips,
and have been greatly extended by the present proprietors. During
the seventy years of their existence a large village has sprung up
around them, until now the settlement is only second to Princetown in size, while it has much more importance as an industrial
centre. Where a little over two generations ago scarcely anything

beyond some farm enclosures in the valley of the Torry, and vestiges of old mining operations, was to be seen, are now abundant evidences of modern enterprise. On a desolate moor traversed only by a few wayfarers journeying between the South Hams and Tavistock, and near where they forded the stream now spanned by the little bridge under Tolchmoor Gate, or looked for the ancient cross to assure themselves they had not strayed from the track, are now rows of substantial cottages and gardens.

About 400 clay labourers are employed at, and around, Lee Moor, by far the greater number of them in the works of Messrs Martin. Fully 100 of these live at Lee Moor, and with their wives and families constitute the inhabitants of the village. Their average wage is from 18s to 20s a week, but this is supplemented in various ways. They cultivate the strip of garden attached to their cottages, and the majority of them also rent allotments, in which they grow potatoes, or a crop of mangolds. Many own pigs, or a cow or two, and nearly all rear poultry, while a number of them have ponies running on the moor. With these advantages they are by no means entirely dependent on their wages, and it is certain there is no other community on Dartmoor better circumstanced. Entirely a settlement of labourers, there is yet an air of prosperity about Lee Moor. A member of the United Kingdom Alliance might possibly be inclined to attribute much of this to the fact that no licensed house exists in the village, that no intoxicants are to be obtained nearer than Shaugh on the one side, or Cornwood on the other, each nearly three miles distant. Perhaps he would not be altogether wrong, but to the efforts of Messrs Martin it is mainly due. They have done much to foster a spirit of content among their employees by the interest they have shown in the village, which if not exactly of their creation, has been formed by them out of a very small beginning.

In the days of the first Mr Phillips the spiritual needs of the little community that was springing up around him were met by Sunday services conducted by Wesleyans, and held in Lee Moor House. Preachers sometimes went there from Plymouth, usually walking to Colebrook (for there was then no railway), where a horse would be waiting to convey them to the house. Several years ago a Wesleyan chapel was built, and there are also schools and a mission-room licensed by the Bishop. The latter was built for church services by Mr T. Martin, and was opened in 1889. The donor fitted up the room at no small expense, and generously provided books and hassocks.

The settlement of Lee Moor is one of those places that is seldom disturbed. Though not nearly so far removed from the borders of the moor as Princetown, there is more seclusion there, at all events in the summer. You see much of the 'in-country', it is true, but there is moor all around you, nevertheless. Visitors, of course, find their way to Lee Moor, but in comparison with the number that flock to Princetown during the season they are very few indeed. It is too much trouble to get there, perhaps. We do not know. It may be that, or it is possible a reason is to be found in the fact that three miles is rather a long distance to go for refreshments.

We have said that Lee Moor is seldom disturbed, but it must not be supposed that there is a total absence of excitement. This is supplied on those occasions when the free and independent electors are being invited to record their votes for candidates for various positions of honour. An old clay labourer once said to me : 'Yes, they com' out to see us thoose times—lots o' mun, an' very often there's a purty to-do. They'm lookin' after us then sharp enough, but when 'tis all over they daun't knaw where us live.'

Many of the clay labourers, like some who work in the granite quarries, can hardly be called Dartmoor men, since they do not dwell on, or quite close to the moor. Those settled at Lee Moor, and the Shaugh men, can, of course, be so regarded, but the others, with the exception of those who live so far away as Plympton, are borderers, and chiefly belong to Cornwood, Lutton, or Meavy. Some know little of Dartmoor, except that part of it in the immediate vicinity of the scene of their labours, while others are well acquainted with the commons lying between the Mew and the Erme, and a few have even a wider knowledge.

F

A supply of water for the Lee Moor clay works is brought from the Plym by means of a leat about three miles in length. The intake is just above Ditsworthy warren house, and the water is conducted across a part of Hen Tor warren, and through Trowlsworthy warren to the reservoir near Lee Moor House. The Torry water is also utilised. This stream has its source at a spot known as White-hill Yeo, below Pen Beacon, and quite near to its springs a very large deposit of clay is now being worked. It is washed through a tunnel from the bottom of the deep excavation that has been made.

The clay raised at the Lee Moor works is dispatched to the Cattewater, where it is shipped, by a railway connecting the pits with the quays. This line crosses the roads leading from Loughtor Mill and from Colebrook to Shaugh, and after passing through Cann Wood reaches Plym Bridge, from which point it keeps close to the Tavistock & Launceston railway nearly to Marsh Mills. An engine is employed on the higher part of this railway, that is to say from the pits to near Plym Bridge, but below the latter the wagons are drawn by horses. Every day a number of wagons pass over this line laden with the product of the Lee Moor pits. Roughly speaking, this amounts to about 60,000 tons a year.

According to a recent article by Mr Herbert Russell in the *Daily Express*, the quantity of clay annually sent from Devon and Cornwall is 603,896 tons, to produce which it is said that at least three million tons of natural clay has to be dug. According to this proportion the 60,000 tons of marketable Dartmoor clay would represent the digging of no less than 300,000 tons.

But what is produced at Lee Moor does not all leave the works in the form of clay. Quite early in their history fire-bricks were made there, and the manufacture of these, and of china stone, still forms an important feature of the industry. Barrel clay is also sent from the works, and this needs the employment there of coopers.

The first part of the clay labourer's work is that of digging the clay from the sides of the pit, for which purpose picks and shovels are used. After the surface covering, or 'burden', is removed the clay is laid bare, and as the deposit is often of considerable thickness the pits are generally very deep. A stream of water is then directed over the clay, and this washes it down to the settling pits, before reaching which, however, it has to pass through the 'dregs', where the sand and mica with which the natural clay is mixed are deposited. From the settling pits it passes into the tanks and thence into buildings, where it is dried by artificial heat. When sufficiently dry it is cut into blocks, and is then ready for the market. The 'cutter' is a sort of crooked knife affixed to the end of a pole.

The 'dregs' have to be cleaned out each evening, and the mica removed. A quantity of clay is also deposited there, but of an inferior quality to that carried forward by the stream. This is washed down to another set of settling pits, and treated in the same manner as the best clay.

When the labourer cleans out his 'dregs' he uses what he calls a 'shiver' for the purpose. This may be likened to an enormous rake without teeth, and is of the same width—about three feet— as the compartments into which the 'dregs' is divided. Boots reaching to the knee are worn when this work is being performed.

The quarrying of granite and the production of clay have proved the most stable of the Dartmoor industries, and the spirit of enterprise which marks those now connected with them furnishes an assurance that they will continue to prosper.

A correspondent remarks that I said nothing in my article on 'The Miner' about the Golden Dagger Mine. Had I been writing on Dartmoor mining in general, I should, of course, have noticed it, but my observations had to do with the worker rather than with the works, and just at present it can hardly be said that the mine is in operation. I am aware that until quite recently it has been working, and previous to the starting of the Hexworthy Mine it was for several years the only one on Dartmoor at which anything was done. Since 1879 it has been worked by Mr Moses Bawden, who during the twenty-four years has paid close upon £20,000 for labour there. At times from thirty to forty miners have been employed.

WHORTLEBERRY GATHERING

OFTEN in the early morning of a fine day in July or August small parties of women and children, and sometimes of men, carrying baskets, may be seen making their way from the villages on the borders of the moor towards the hills. There is generally more of a holiday look about them than one suggestive of labour, and yet their time is not to be idly spent. They will work hard enough before the sun goes down, though the task will be regarded as a pleasure nevertheless. They are going to gather whortleberries, or as they themselves would tell you, they are 'gwain to moor, pickin' hurts'.

The whortleberry (*Vaccinium myrtillus*) grows in great abundance on Dartmoor, and while large quantities are annually gathered there, it is equally certain that much larger quantities are 'born to blush unseen'. The season usually commences early in July, and lasts about two months, and there is not a border village in which a day or two on the moor to gather the berries is not looked forward to as a holiday. The people of each village have their favourite locale for gathering, and they seldom go in search of the berries anywhere else. On the southern verge of the moor, that is to say, from the Yealm to the Avon, a combe known as Stony Bottom is in great repute. A small tributary of the Erme, called Hook Lake, runs through the combe, which is almost entirely covered with the debris of an old stream work. Over this the whortleberry plants have spread themselves, and they also grow on the sides of the combe, and on the heath around it. If you were to ask any of those gatherers who go from Brent, or its neighbourhood, to name a spot in their locality where the berries were always plentiful they would mention Stony Bottom.

At Princetown the whortleberry season is not looked forward to with that eagerness with which it is anticipated in the villages on the confines of the waste. One probable reason for this is that 'a day to moor' would be much less attractive to the dwellers there than to the border villagers; and another is, perhaps, to be found in the different conditions of its people. In the villages old customs still survive; they have been continued from father to son for generations. But many of the inhabitants of Princetown are not natives of the moor, and do not heed its traditions. Whortleberry gathering would not be regarded as a pleasure, and being for the most part well circumstanced, they do not need to do it for profit. Those that do go, however, generally find their way to Omen Beam, as the tract of ground lying to the northward of the road leading from Rundle Stone to Two Bridges is called. This part has always been noted for the abundance of the whortleberry plant, and is referred to in that connection in a brief account of the moor written nearly sixty years ago by Miss Sophie Dixon, who lived for some time at Princetown. She states that she had counted upwards of five hundred gatherers on Omen Beam at one time, so that formerly, at all events, Princetown must have furnished its quota of those who went in quest of the purple berries. With regard to this name we have adopted the form employed at present, and which appears on the latest Ordnance map, but in Moore's *History of Devonshire*, in a note giving a list of certain mines furnished by Mr John Taylor to the brothers Lysons, it appears as Holming Beam, and as such it is given by Miss Dixon.

From Mary Tavy and Lydford the gatherers go chiefly to the upper part of the Doe Tor Brook, and to the slope of Hare Tor, above Tavy Cleave. The little valley in which the brook named takes its rise is formed by the ridge extending from Links Tor to Hare Tor on one side, and on the other by that on which Arms Tor and Bra Tor are placed. It is known in the neighbourhood as Foxholes, from a mine of that name which formerly existed there, the remains of which may still be seen. Below Hare Tor the ground is much strewn with rocks. These afford good shelter for the whortleberry plants, which here grow very luxuriantly. This area is constantly visited by gatherers during the season, but so abundant is the fruit there that day after day they are able to return with a plentiful supply. When after several weeks of gathering the berries do begin to grow scarce, there are those who penetrate further into the moor, to spots where the plants are still laden with the fruit. Foxholes is about six miles from Mary Tavy but the pickers think little of such a distance provided it brings them to a spot where there is no lack of berries. During the past wet season the walk has often been a useless one, for the gatherers have arrived at their destination only to find that their hopes of a fine day were not to be fulfilled, and have been obliged to return with empty baskets and drenched to the skin.

In some parts of the moor, such as at Dark Lake, in the south quarter of the Forest, and on the northern slope of Fur Tor, the plants so thickly cover the ground that it is possible to gather a very large quantity in a comparatively short time. These spots, however, are not usually visited. They are too remote, and, as already observed, it is only those who when the berries become scarce in those places generally resorted to, are yet desirous of obtaining more, that venture so far out. Around Walkham Head whortleberries also grow in immense quantities, but this, too, is a spot to which the gatherer does not often go. One may stand in the old turf ties there, long since overgrown with herbage, and, the ground between the pits being three or four feet above their surface, gather the fruit without stooping. Very many places might be named where whortleberries grow in plenty; indeed, it is impossible to be anywhere on Dartmoor, except on the great tracts of fen, without being near spots covered with the plants.

These journeys to gather whortleberries have given many of the people in the villages a knowledge of the moor, or at all events of that part of it in the neighbourhood of their homes, that they would never otherwise have possessed. The duties of the men may often take them there, but the women and children having no occasion to visit it, the probability is that they would never do so were there no whortleberries to gather. But the six or eight miles walk over the common, the route being sometimes varied, a long day amid the tors, and this perhaps repeated several times during the summer, gives them after a few seasons some acquaintance with their own quarter of the moor at least. We know country-women who are quite familiar with certain parts of Dartmoor, and have gained all their knowledge of it by going there year after year to gather whortleberries.

Although by the majority of the villagers a day on the moor for this purpose is regarded more in the light of a holiday than anything else, there are some with whom gain is the sole motive for going there. These go out perhaps two or three times a week throughout the season, and the quantities they gather are often very large. One family in the parish of Mary Tavy, consisting of father, mother, and daughter, and who have been regularly to the moor for whortleberries for many years, have during the past season gathered sufficient to give them a return of £9. The berries were mostly sold at Tavistock, and fetched 6d and 7d a quart. One lot was sold at 5d, and some few lots made as much as 8d, but the average was as stated. On one day the two women gathered 26 quarts between them, and on another occasion the father gathered a like quantity unassisted, and this he did within twelve hours, including a walk of about a dozen miles. On Omen Beam this season a man and his wife and child gathered 38 quarts in one day, and other large gatherings have also come to our notice.

It is said that a drink made from the whortleberry is sold in the streets of St Petersburg. The fruit is also sometimes used for making a kind of cordial here. This is known as 'hurt gin', and the mode of preparing it is similar to that followed in making sloe gin. But it is not considered to be equal to the latter. A dish of stewed whortleberries, however, or a tart made from them, nobody can find fault with, and it is in such a manner that they are generally used.

It is rather curious to note the different customs observed in the villages round the moor by the gatherers. In the southern part it is quite the usual thing for each to carry a small can—often one that holds exactly a quart—as well as a basket. As the berries are picked they are put into the can, and when it will hold no more it is emptied into the basket. By this means the gatherer can tell if he chooses what quantity of fruit he has, and he also finds it easier to move about, especially if the ground be thickly strewn with rocks, with only a small can than with a good-sized basket. But in the northern part of the moor the can is very seldom seen. The berries are thrown into the basket as they are gathered, and the quantity is measured on the gatherer's arrival at home.

The words, too, formerly uttered by the whortleberry picker in southern Dartmoor, when commencing to gather, and considered so essential to the success of his endeavours to fill his basket, we have never been able to meet with elsewhere. Readers of *The River* will remember how Hannah Bradridge, when she went whortle-berry gathering with Mary Merle, did not forget to speak them—

> The first I pick, I eat;
> The second I pick, I throw away;
> The third I pick, I put in my can—

and how she followed this up with the observation.

'There, Molly, now us shall have good hurting.' We first heard these lines about thirty years ago, but even then those who used them did not appear to place too much reliance upon the charm.

The red whortleberry is not unknown on Dartmoor, though so far as we are aware it is found only in one place there. The spot is a very remote one, which those who would regret the extermina-tion of the plant will regard as fortunate. The botanist in search of specimens may not be quite so bad a sinner as the man who shoots some very rare bird and then trumpets the fact abroad as though it were something to be proud of instead of being an act to be condemned, but he is nevertheless capable of destroying much.

The name by which the Devonshire peasant knows the whortle-berry is found in heraldry, and thus has the respectability of antiquity. The hurt, or hurte as it is sometimes written, is one of the five roundels of the colours.[1] It is azure, but as the five

[1] There are two other roundels of the colours, but they are rarely encountered.

roundels are globular it is shaded. Fuller in speaking of the fruit mentions that the arms of the Baskervilles, of Herefordshire, showed a chevron between three hurts proper.

While some of the gatherers, as we have seen, contrive to make a substantial addition to their income during the whortleberry season, there are none but what get much more than the amount of a day's ordinary earnings for their trouble. The small sums made by the children of the poorer of the villagers are often very helpful, and as their holidays take place during the period the berries are ripe, the 'day to moor' does not cause any absence from school.

A day with the hurt pickers—not as a gatherer, perhaps, for that exercise might be found rather tedious—is most enjoyable, especially if there happen to be some aged labourer among the party who has 'heerd tell' of certain things that happened 'years agone'. It is a picnic of the most unconvential character, and given sunny skies there is music in it from beginning to end. The picker leaves all his cares behind him—they are usually not very weighty ones—and gives himself up to the matter that has called him to the moor. The more youthful of the party are in high spirits, and the merry prattle of the children is heard all through the livelong day. And Nature comes forward to add to the pleasing sounds. An unseen songster carols overhead, and the stream sings to you from below. With all this ringing in your ears you scramble over grey boulders that the whortleberry plants partly hide, or take your ease upon some patch of short turf, hemmed in by tall bracken. By-and-by the sun tells the gatherers it is time to start upon their homeward way, and with well-filled baskets they turn their faces towards the village that lies beyond the hill over which the evening shadows are fast creeping. You reach home and rest, and in your dreams that night may perhaps see a group of women and children carrying baskets and threading their way between masses of rock, or passing knee-deep through heather. But whether you do or not, it is certain that your memory will never fail to carry you back to a certain happy day when you 'went to moor pickin' hurts'.

THE SPORTSMAN

SO many-sided is Dartmoor that it has something to offer to all, and while it is a fine field for the archaeologist, the student of folklore, the artist, the geologist, and the botanist, it is none the less so for the hunting man and the angler. It is, indeed, as a hunting ground that we first hear of it, and during the seven hundred years that have passed since that time it is unlikely that there has ever been a period when it has ceased to be such. Formerly it was the stag that was hunted on Dartmoor, but he was exterminated considerably more than a century ago, and now, except for an occasional straggler from Exmoor, he is not seen there. A few years since there were some hopes that Dartmoor might again become a stag-hunting country, though Mr C. H. Basset, a former Master of Staghounds, gave it as his opinion that an endeavour to make it so would not be attended with success. Dartmoor was more boggy, and consequently a more difficult country than Exmoor, he said, and he also doubted whether the south Devon farmers would look as favourably upon it as those of Exmoor, who had been born to stag-hunting. The opinion of such an authority cannot, of course, be disregarded, but there are nevertheless those who think that the sport might be revived.

But although the kingly pursuit of hunting the red deer is no longer followed on Dartmoor, many a good run at the tail of a pack of hounds takes place there. Foxhounds and harriers regularly hunt all parts of the moor, and if their quarry be not so noble as the antlered stag, it at all events demands as much nerve and skill to follow the former as were required in the days when a deer was roused in the woods round Holne, or the coverts of Lydford, and went away at a racing pace towards the open Forest. Riding to hounds in the in-country and a run on Dartmoor are two very

The Sportsman Daniel Leaman of Dartmeet, 9 October 1888. 'A great fisherman; not innocent, so it is said, of occasional poaching'. So reads the caption in Robert Burnard's album

Under Canvas The 1873 autumn army manœuvres. The camp of the 1st Division on south-west Dartmoor

different things, as those who find themselves galloping over the moor after a game fox for the first time are ready enough to admit. It is true there are no banks, but the obstacles, though not so apparent as in the cultivated country, are very much more real. To ride over Dartmoor requires a knowledge of the country, and a horse that is accustomed to it. The first is absolutely essential if the rider is to keep up with the hounds and at the same time avoid the bogs. Strangers sometimes adopt the expedient of 'following somebody' familiar with the ground—a very good plan, perhaps, if it could always be carried out, but the failure of which is not unlikely to lead to disappointing results.

The run with Mr Sperling's hounds in January 1889, when so many of the field came to grief in the mire under Mis Tor, may not exactly be an example of what Dartmoor hunting usually is, but it at all events shows what may happen when the line is carried over treacherous ground, or across the fen. The meet was at Woodtown, and on Heckwood and Partown Wood being drawn a fox was found in the latter. Some little time elapsed before the pack could be got on, but they picked up the $2\frac{1}{2}$ couple of hounds which had carried the line by King Tor, near Long Ash Brook, where there was a check. This enabled the field to come up, and when the hounds hit off the line pointing for Mis Tor the riders were on good terms with them. The fox was seen on the northern side of the tor, and beyond this the hounds crossed the Walkham, and running up the gully on the west side recrossed the stream at the point where it is forded by an old track known as the Lych Path, and running eastward were lost in the valley of the Cowsic. Here two couple of hounds came up, and being cheered on by Mr Sperling, Spiller, the huntsman, and the whip, soon hit off the line of a fox and carried it up the valley and out on to the fen. It being impossible to ride over this, four of the field undertook to take charge of the horses, which had now dwindled to ten in number, while their riders followed in the wake of the hounds on foot. On reaching the East Dart they found that the fox was not the one the pack was hunting, and they therefore made their way to Two Bridges. Hearing nothing of the horses there, search had to be made for them, but the four in whose charge they had been left were not met with until fog and darkness covered the moor. Then it was found that four of the horses had broken away, and these had to remain on the moor until the following day.

A number of the field got no further than Mis Tor Mire. Here Miss Spearman, of Plymouth, in attempting to jump the prison leat which runs through it, was thrown, her horse sinking deeply into the mire. The Rev Clifford Rickards, at that time chaplain of the prison, immediately went to her assistance, while Mr Crockford, a veteran sportsman, rode rapidly to Merivale Bridge to obtain the aid required to extricate the horse. Returning with men and ropes, they set about the work, but it was some time before the animal was rescued. The only lady who reached the Cowsic was Miss Sybil Collier.

It was afterwards found that the fox instead of having taken up the Cowsic valley, as had been imagined, had run down it, and turning right and running under Mis Tor had gone nearly to Merivale. From here he went back to Partown Wood, ran down the Walkham valley to Ward Bridge, and the back of Woodtown on to Bicklime Wood, where he was left.

Seventy years ago 'Silver-tailed Billy', the Dewer Stone fox, showed capital sport over Dartmoor, and the game 'varmints' that are still found there prove clearly enough that he and his brethren left sons and daughters who have not failed to increase and multiply. Some wonderful performances are chronicled by the older sportsmen, but they do not throw the runs of recent years into the shade. A run of twelve or thirteen miles to their only check, the greater part of the distance through cover, and over some of the roughest part of Dartmoor, is no small matter for hounds to accomplish, but such performances are not unknown. A few years ago the South Devons found an old dog fox in the plantations at Brimpts, and after rattling him right through to Lough Tor Heath, he turned, and entering the cover again, passed Brimpts House, and made away for the West Dart, which he crossed just below Hexworthy Bridge. From the river he passed up over the moor towards Combestone Tor, and leaving that pile on his right ran through the rough and stony covers under Bench Tor. The pace was a clinking one, and only four or five of the best mounted had the satisfaction of catching a sight of the hounds. Finding himself hard pressed in the stock covers, the fox broke, but being headed at Holne Moor Gate turned back to Holne Cot Wood. Through this he ran to New Bridge and over Chase Hill to Holne Park lawn, where there was a check—one hour and ten minutes from the find. He was afterwards killed near the Raven Rock, in Buckland Woods.

A 'clinker' with the harriers is also a thing by no means unknown. A jack which was found by the Dart Vales in the Cowsic valley, a little above Two Bridges, went off like a shot from a gun up the hill to Longaford Tor, and passing White Tor, crossed the Powder Mills bog to the Moreton road. Racing across Muddy Lakes newtake, he made away for Bellaford Tor, and then turned back to the newtake again. From there he ran into the enclosures belonging to Prince Hall, and crossed the West Dart to Round Hill, and on to Bair Down and Wistman's Wood. Thence he ran over the hill, pointing once more for the Powder Mills bog, but turned sharp back to Two Bridges, where he again crossed the river. There the hounds ran into him, after a run of three-quarters of an hour without a single check.

The otter is also hunted in the Dartmoor rivers, there being several packs of hounds kept for the purpose. On certain parts of the rivers on the borders of the moor it is rough going, both for the hounds and those who follow them, and in this respect the hunting is unlike that further down stream, where the waters are smooth and deep, and level meadows form the banks. The otter is rather scarce, but speaking generally the packs show good sport, and there are usually fairly large fields.

It is hardly necessary to say that game is scarce on Dartmoor. Some years ago the black grouse was preserved there by Sir

Robert Torrens, whose shooting rights extended over that part of the south quarter of the Forest bounded by the West Dart and the Swincombe, Plym Head, Fish Lake Foot, the Avon, the northern boundary of Huntingdon warren, the West Wellabrook, and the manor of Holne. This bird is still found on the moor, though it is by no means abundant. The Rev E. Adrian Woodruffe-Peacock, consulting soil and grass specialist, of Brigg, Lincolnshire, in a recent communication to us, expresses the opinion that black game would do well on Dartmoor. There are certain difficulties in the way of its preservation, perhaps, but these might not prove insuperable.

Several birds, as well as quadrupeds, which formerly existed on the moor, are now seldom, or never, seen there, which is scarcely to be wondered at, seeing that when a species is becoming rare, instead of endeavours being made to preserve it, every specimen that is observed is too often eagerly shot at, in order that it may be stuffed and placed in somebody's collection. Thus we sometimes read that such-and-such a bird, formerly very common, is now only occasionally met with, but that a few specimens have been lately obtained.

It was formerly said that the golden eagle made its nest on the Dewer Stone, but Howard, in his poem of 'Bickleigh Vale', published in 1804, although he mentions several birds and animals as haunting that crag, availing himself possibly of the licence usually accorded to a poet, makes no allusion to that bird. It was, however, stated to have been seen by a visitor to Hey Tor in May 1891, and as he had come across the golden eagle in the Alps, and was once given a specimen of one which had been shot by a Swiss chamois hunter in the Bernese Oberland, he must be allowed to know something of the bird. Mr M. U. J. Teil, of Wolborough, Newton Abbot, a well-known naturalist, was not inclined to dispute the fact that it had been seen, but there were others who suggested that the visitor may have been mistaken, and that the bird he had observed was the white-tailed eagle. It has, however, been stated that although somewhat of a 'rara avis', the golden eagle is seen more often in England than is generally supposed.

The buzzard was formerly much more common on Dartmoor than at present. It has been sometimes thought that this is a very solitary bird, and that it is an extremely rare circumstance for more than two to be seen together. This, however, is not the case, for as many as five have been seen in company in the Lustleigh valley, and the late Prebendary Wolfe once counted thirteen settling down on the tor behind his house at Leighon. Buzzards breed in the neighbourhood, and Prebendary Wolfe had observed their nests. Mr A. R. Hunt, of Torquay, has also observed these birds, which fly, he says, in pairs, and are sometimes accompanied by their young. Buzzards have also been seen in Buckland Woods.

Prebendary Wolfe has also stated that ravens breed about Hey Tor. Fox Tor, in the south quarter of the Forest, is a favourite haunt of those birds, and they may often be seen there during the hot summer days.

For the angler Dartmoor possesses a particular attraction. The number of its streams is so great that in whatever part of the moor he may be he is always within easy reach of one, and on all of them good trout fishing may be obtained. Many of the Dartmoor natives are good fishermen, but the older of those who loved to cast a fly upon the waters have passed away during the last eight or ten years. Born and reared in that land of streams, they know the most likely spots to afford sport, and being keen observers of the state of the weather and the water, can tell the most killing fly to use on all occasions. Men like Daniel Leaman or Will Mann could always depend upon filling their baskets with trout, and if there were salmon in the Dart, knew where to find them. Their flies they made themselves, and that was the only part of their tackle they took any trouble about. A pliant rod or a silk and hair line was a matter of no moment to them. They could make a cast with a rod as stiff as a hop pole as well as most fishermen with an expensive Copham, and as for their line—well, it cost them threepence 'in to Ashburton'. The moor knows them no longer, but there are younger men who may not be deemed unworthy successors.

Most of the Dartmoor streams are preserved by fishing associations, and licences are necessary to fish them. These can be obtained in the towns and larger villages round the moor.

The Dartmoor trout are not large, but they are brave and lusty, and the number a fisherman may kill in a day more than compensates for their comparatively small size. It has been sought to obtain Parliamentary powers to impose a size limit for trout fishing generally, but it is difficult to see how such could act fairly. A trout that would be deemed small on some rivers would be regarded as a fine fish on a Dartmoor stream, and the matter seems to be one entirely for local authorities to deal with.

Some capital baskets have been taken during the past season, notwithstanding that the weather was so much against the sport. Salmon have seldom been so plentiful. In one district on the Dart 195 fish were taken by 26 rods. Mr J. Martin, of Moorlands, accounted for 46 of these, the largest number captured by one fisherman. One fish, which he caught in April last, turned the scale at $17\frac{1}{2}$ lb, after having been out of the water for twenty-four hours.

When the breath of spring sweeps lightly over the moor, and Nature begins to awaken from her hibernal sleep, the angler looks with an eager eye towards its streams; when the summer has faded and winter is about to hold the waste in his grip, the hunter passes to the hills with hound and horn; and so old Dartmoor finds something for the sportsman's hand to do throughout the long year.

UNDER CANVAS

PROBABLY the first to pitch their tents on Dartmoor were the gipsies, and they may still be seen at times on its verge. Their example has been followed by those on pleasure bent, who find in a short sojourn under canvas much enjoyment. A good deal of this is derived from the novelty of camping out, and also as affording an excellent means of seeing the moor. Others who for a time 'dwell in tents' on the waste are the soldiers who annually encamp there, and the volunteers, Dartmoor having during several years past been the scene of military operations.

The earliest encampment of troops on the moor of which there is any record, so far as I can discover, was formed on Hemerdon Ball, in the parish of Plympton St Mary, in the beginning of the nineteenth century, when an invasion by Napoleon was deemed not unlikely. Tradition, however, comes forward with an account of a still earlier encampment on the moor, not of soldiers, but of women and children. These, it is said, were sent there from Plymouth at a time when the French were almost hourly expected to enter the harbour, in order to ensure their safety. In August 1779, the French and Spanish fleets appeared off Plymouth, and remained in sight for several days, capturing an English vessel and destroying a number of Cawsand fishing-boats. Great consternation seems to have prevailed in the town, and it is probable that the story has its foundation in this incident. Some evidence of this is afforded by a musical farce by Dibdin, a Mr Neville being responsible for the words, which was produced in the same year at Covent Garden Theatre. Its title is *Plymouth in an Uproar*, and it has for its subject the much-feared invasion. The townspeople are shown as being considerably alarmed, a report having spread that the enemy had landed at Maker. Everybody is anxious to get out of the town as quickly as possible, and one

G

of the places named as being likely to afford a refuge is Dart-moor.

Over forty years ago there was an encampment on the common to the northward of Butterdon Hill, near Ivybridge. The ground marked out for rifle practice was situated near the green path leading from Harford Gate to Owley, and here butts were erected, and granite shelters for the markers. Of these the remains of eight, forming two rows, still exist.

Lines of tents were to be seen in several parts of the moor during the period of the autumn manœuvres of 1873. Wet weather, however, prevailed, and for the greater part of the time life under canvas was by no means an agreeable experience. The appearance in their midst of the military was regarded as an important event by the natives of the moor, and for some time it was customary to fix the date of any particular circumstance by stating that it occurred either so many years before, or after, 'the sojers was out heer', as the case might be. Jonas Coaker, so well known on the moor as a maker of verses, was particularly interested in the operations, his enthusiasm finding vent in a long string of rhymes in which he described the various regiments that took part in them.

Since the establishment of the artillery camp near Okehampton, the population of Dartmoor during about five months in the year is considerably increased. It is true that the camping ground is situated on the very verge of the moor, but it is within its confines, nevertheless. The firing zone embraces a considerable tract, includ-ing Okehampton Common and a large portion of the north quarter of the Forest. Yet such is the size of Dartmoor that many miles of wild country intervene between it and those parts of the waste in which most of the farms are situated.

The camp occupies a site at the foot of Black Down Hill, an eminence forming a part of the ancient Park of Okehampton, and here a number of buildings necessary to it, and long lines of sheds for horses, have been erected. Near these the tents are pitched. Access to the camp is gained by a steep road from Okehampton railway station, but it is stated that the construction of a loop line from near Meldon, directly into it, is in contemplation. The batteries that visit the camp for practice during the summer usually remain for a few weeks, and if the weather is fine the men have a very agreeable time. Upon this, of course, the comfort of camp life everywhere depends, but an inclement season is particularly to be dreaded on Dartmoor.

The firing zone extends from the Sourton Tors, on the west, to Watchet Hill, on the east, and is marked at various points by danger boards. There is one of these on the hill above Sourton church; another at the northern end of Amicombe Hill, near Kitty Tor; one on Great Kneeset; one near Cranmere Pool, which is just within the zone; and others between that point and Watchet Hill. On this eminence, which rises above the village of Belstone, a red flag is hoisted one hour before firing commences, and is kept flying during its continuance, and another is similarly hoisted on Yes Tor. Practice begins early, and is usually ended by about two o'clock, so that ramblers in this part of the moor may generally depend on finding the ground within the zone open to them after that hour.

Firing takes place for the most part on Halstock Down, which lies to the southward of the eastern end of the park, the targets being fixed near East Mill Tor and on Ockment Hill. The Down is conterminous with the Forest, according to the boundary now recognised, and immediately within the latter, and in the angle formed by the Black-a-ven Brook and the East Ockment, is the only enclosed land on the range, or indeed within the firing zone. This belongs to East Ockment farm, the lease of which has been acquired by the War Office. As shells are fired directly over the farmhouse, an underground shelter has been provided into which the inmates can retire on the commencement of practice, a very necessary arrangement, seeing that, although the dwelling is below the line of fire, the chimney was on one occasion struck by a shot.

The targets consist of wooden figures of men, both fixed and movable. These represent infantry either in standing or lying positions, and cavalry in the act of charging. There are also dummy guns, with limbers and wagons, the practice being carried out under conditions as nearly as possible resembling those of actual warfare. So realistic are the dummies that they reply by harmless fire. This is contrived by a member of the staff, who is concealed in a splinter-proof shelter, from which he produces an effect very like the flash of a field-gun. Sometimes during the action the senior non-commissioned officer of a gun will be informed that he is a 'casualty' that is, that he is supposed to be wounded. He then drops on one knee, after which he rises, and taking off his haversack, proceeds to the rear, his place at the gun being at once taken by a junior. The chief umpire awards marks to the batteries according to their merits, and every non-commissioned officer and man of the best six of these wear badges, which are retained until the list of prizes is published for the following year. This plan of conducting the practice in a manner as much like real warfare as is possible has proved not only successful in rendering the men efficient gunners, but excellent as bringing them acquainted with the kind of work they would be called upon to perform in the field.

During the past season the weather has not been favourable to gunnery practice on Dartmoor. Wet days have been frequent, and a mist has often hung over the moor. Practice was interferred with to such an extent that there were rumours in the camp during September that instead of breaking up as usual early in October, it would continue until the end of the month. But the weather showing no signs of improvement practice was not extended. Earl Roberts visited the camp in September, and witnessed some experiments, including the testing of a new quick-firing gun, and some different kinds of shell, as well as of some gun-carriages and motor vehicles.

The volunteer camp, which has been often formed on Hey Tor Down, on the eastern side of the moor, was stationed there for the first time in 1884, when the various companies comprising the 5th Devon Regiment assembled for eight days' instruction. Before that date it had been customary to choose a camping ground in the vicinity of one or other of those towns which furnished the regiment with men; but when these had all been visited, it was considered that a fixed place for the encampment would be desirable. Hey Tor Down, about four miles from Bovey Tracey, and four and a half from Ashburton, was after much consideration selected, and the choice of the executive was one that commended itself to all. The camp was planned on a tract of ground between Hey Tor and Saddle Tor, and consisted of seven lines of bell-shaped tents, about eleven in each line, together with officers' tents, and tents for supplies. Close to Saddle Tor was a large marquee forming the canteen, which was in charge of Sergeant Doble and Corporal G. Bearne, of Newton Abbot. A part of the marquee was set aside for entertainments, and in these the Ashburton handbell ringers took an appreciable part.

On the Sunday, which was the second day in camp, service was conducted on the ground by the chaplain, the late Rev G. T. Warner, of Newton, when a total of 418 of all ranks assembled. This was rather over two-thirds of the full strength of the regiment, but the numbers were augmented during the week, over 500 being present at the inspection.

When the last year of the century arrived the Hey Tor camp presented a very different appearance from that which it wore when it was first stationed on the down. Instead of there being no more than eighty or ninety tents, hundreds were to be seen, and on the first Sunday when a service was conducted by Prebendary Dr Dangar, of the Exeter Training College, and the Rev B. B. Liptrott, vicar of St George's Church, Stonehouse, the total force in camp was estimated to be about 3,500 rank and file, including 250 cyclists. The period of encampment was not for a week only as in the earlier years, but for a month; most of the men came in for a fortnight, and some remained during the whole time.

Great preparations had to be made, and traction engines were employed to bring stores to the ground. All the tents were floored, the Government having provided this luxury in consequence of the prolonged stay, and the men were supplied with straw mattresses. Two large marquees were set aside for purposes of recreation, and for reading and writing, one of them being erected by the YMCA. There was a post-office, a hospital, and transport offices, and the headquarters were connected with the stables and the range by telephone. The regiments in camp were the 1st, 2nd, 4th, and 5th DR, and the 1st and 2nd DCLI.

Hey Tor Down may be an ideal place for a camp in fine weather, but when the storm-cloud bursts upon the moor there are others that might be considered preferable. For a tent to be blown off the camping ground, and carried to such a distance as to be not readily recoverable, is a thing not altogether unknown there. An experience of this kind, particularly when the rain is descending in torrents, might possibly damp the ardour of anyone less enthusiastic than a British volunteer. He simply makes the best he can of it, and resolves that in future he will give a little more attention to his tent-pegging.

Other parts of the moor are also occasionally selected as camping grounds. In the summer of 1888 there was a combined camp of regulars and volunteers on Roborough Down, but the bad weather interfered very much with the various exercises. On the last day, however, when the battle of Cadaford Bridge was fought, the sun shone brilliantly, and the mimic engagement took place under most favourable conditions. The general idea was that a hostile force was marching on Plymouth from the north, four battalions of infantry and half a company of mounted infantry being under orders to cross the Mew, march on Cadaford Bridge, and thence by the road past Collard to the banks of the Plym. The main body of the defenders were in position across the Tavistock and Plymouth road south of Bickleigh. The attacking force was under the command of Col E. L. England, the defending force being commanded by Col F. Freemantle. Gen Lyons, to whom the reports of the umpires were handed, gave the attacking force the advantage.

About one thousand militia troops, under the command of Lt

Col H. C. Eagles, went into camp on Yennadon Down in the summer of 1900. The camp consisted of nearly two hundred marquees and service tents, but as the men only remained under canvas for a week the arrangements were not particularly elaborate.

Twenty years have elapsed since the 'Dartmoor Irregulars' went into camp near King Tor, on Walkhampton Common. The force was a small one, numbering only four, the 'colonel', the 'major', the 'lieutenant', and the 'cook', the latter being regarded as by far the most important member of the company. The accommodation was ample, there being three tents for the four individuals. One of these was used for the stores, another was for sleeping in, and the third was set apart as a kind of recreation tent. A few mishaps were encountered, such as the pole of a tent going through the canvas, and the loss of a ham, and all the bacon and butter, to which an uninvited guest had helped himself. To prevent a recurrence of such a serious matter the 'colonel's' retriever was sent for, and put on sentry duty at the store tent. A very enjoyable time was spent, and the last night in camp was celebrated by the lighting of a large bonfire.

We have ourselves camped out on Dartmoor, both with a tent and without one. In the latter case a turf tie or a gully has afforded shelter. The latest instance of camping out on the moor that we know of is that of a scissor-grinder, who, at the end of April last, was living in a small gipsy tent in the neighbourhood of Princetown.

THE PRISON OFFICER

DARTMOOR is at once synonymous with freedom and with captivity. In no part of our country has the hand of man gained less ascendancy over primeval Nature than in this western upland, where bright streams sing through the long summer day to hills that still wear the garb they put on ages ago, and yet in its midst is a spot where men bewail their lost liberty. To most of us the name of this wild region awakens thoughts of breezy heights, from which grey tors rise in stern and rugged grandeur, of heathery slopes and ferny hollows, and of rivers that have their course through deep and narrow valleys; to some it means only a place of bondage. For rather over half a century has the old war prison at Princetown, less than five miles from the centre of the moor, been used as a depot for convicts. The home of freedom has become, by the irony of fate, the site of one of thraldom's grim abodes.

In the year following the peace of Waterloo, the captives being set at liberty, the gloomy place of detention on the moor was deserted, and though subsequently used for other purposes, it was not until after the lapse of thirty-five years that prisoners again set foot within its walls. But soon after the gates had been opened to the prisoners of war it was proposed to convert it into a convict depot. The subject is referred to in a report by a Committee of the House of Commons on the Prisons of the Metropolis, in 1818, in which it is stated that evidence had been received that 2,000 convicts might be secured at Dartmoor, and that the cost of adapting the prison to that purpose would not exceed £5,000. The evidence in favour of the proposal is stated in the report, but the Committee, while calling attention to the fact that in the judgment of several respectable witnesses great advantages might be expected from the application of convict labour on Dartmoor, refrained from expressing any opinion on the matter. Proposals were also made to turn the prison into a school of industry for boys from the metropolis, and a public meeting was held in London in 1820 in furtherance of the design. Another suggestion for utilising the buildings was that they should be fitted up as dwellings for settlers, who might employ themselves in cultivating the moor. These schemes were, however, abandoned in turn, but ultimately the earlier one was reverted to, and in 1850, 200 convicts were brought to the moor to execute the work of altering the buildings. The huge prison under North Hisworthy Tor then became a penal settlement, and an occupation entirely new to Dartmoor had its commencement.

In 1883 the Directors of Convict Prisons issued an order whereby the prison at Princetown was advanced to the position of a 'first-class' convict establishment. There were in that year 1,180 convicts confined there, a larger number than had ever been within its walls at one time, and this has probably never been greatly exceeded. At present the number of prisoners is about 1,130, for the purpose of guarding which, and for the work in connection with the establishment, a staff numbering about 250 is required. The latter consists of the Governor, Mr Basil Thomson, the Deputy-Governor, Maj Briscoe, two medical officers, chaplain and Roman Catholic priest, Protestant and Roman Catholic scripture readers, schoolmaster, storekeeper, foreman-of-works, clerks, farm bailiff, chief warder, about 210 warders, and 30 civil guards. About two-thirds of the warders are, like the civil guards, drawn from the army and navy, and are chiefly non-commissioned and petty officers; among the remainder are many farmers' sons, as well as men who are acquainted with certain trades, these being necessary for instructing the prisoners in the different kinds of work to which they are put. There are three instructors, one being a mason, another a carpenter, and another a blacksmith, and these receive additional pay; there is also a warder who has charge of the granite quarry, superintending the work there, which includes the carrying out of blasting operations.

For the purpose of regulating the hours of duty the warders are divided into two groups, known as 'Right' and 'Left'. One goes on duty at 5.30 a.m., when every man has to answer to his name before the Deputy-Governor, or chief warder, and the other at 7 a.m., and these sides change places every morning, each one thus being on early duty on alternate days. They remain on duty for twelve hours, those who commence at 5.30 having intervals for breakfast and dinner, while the others are allowed an interval for dinner only. Night duty is performed entirely by the assistant warders, each one taking his turn. About fifteen are required, and these are constantly visited by a principal warder in company with another warder. There are also two night watchmen, whose duty it is to parade the prison yards during the whole of the night.

That the duties of the prison officer are of a monotonous character need hardly be said, but such is perhaps not the case to so great an extent at Dartmoor as in some other penal establishments. Much of the work of the convicts lies outside the prison walls, and consisting in a large measure of farming operations and the reclamation of land, offers not a little variety. Still, to walk up and down a limited space, keeping watch over a gang of convicts, for hours together, day after day and week after week, as some of the guards have to do, is not a very enviable occupation; nor is that of taking charge of the workshops within the prison, with nothing to look at but a number of men whose hearts must be anywhere rather than in their labour. There is much responsibility attached to the duties of the prison officer, for while attempts to escape are not numerous, there is always a possibility of such being made. Attacks upon warders are unhappily of by no means infrequent occurrence, and the officer has therefore ever to be on the alert. He has to see that the men placed in his charge perform the work assigned to them, at the same time not forgetting that at any moment some untoward circumstance may occur.

But though he finds himself in the midst of so much that is depressing, the life of the prison officer has nevertheless its pleasant side. At Princetown much has been done to render this

The Antiquary Re-erecting the stones at the west end of the Down Tor stone row. The Rev W. A. G. Gray is in charge. Photograph by Robert Burnard, 14 April 1894

The Antiquary The Rev Sabine Baring-Gould supervises the restoration of hut circle no. 3 at Grim's Pound. Photograph by Robert Burnard, 26 May 1894

Coaching A coach excursion about to set off across Dartmoor from the Dolphin Hotel, Bovey Tracey

The Artist William Widgery (1826–1893) photographed on Dartmoor by his friend Richard Gowing, editor of the *Exeter Gazette*

as attractive as possible, and those to whom the moorlands have something to offer more than merely a suitable district to which to deport convicts, find there a desirable place of abode. Long service has also caused some to become so attached to the prison that they have felt genuine sorrow when the time has come for them to retire from the service. Mr Hodge, late chief warder, who was connected with the prison for thirty-five years, was one of these. When, about two years ago, he was retired, he expressed his regrets that he could not remain another year, and said that he loved every stone in the old building in which he had passed so long a time. He still resides at Princetown, and, as a man should be who has lived long years under a Dartmoor sky, is the picture of good health.

Good dwellings are provided by the Government for most of the prison officials, the rent being deducted from the salaries of the occupiers. Others live in the older part of the village, and in the barracks which were originally built for the soldiers who formed the guard over the prisoners of war. The entrance gate to the barrack-yard was removed about forty years ago. Previous to that time no one but those actually residing there was permitted to enter without permission from the sentry, and no tradesman was allowed to sell goods there unless he first obtained the Governor's sanction. All officers, and the members of their families, had to be in at 10 p.m., at which hour the gate was locked, and any who offended by climbing the walls were subject to a penalty. Near the entrance to the barrack-yard the superintendent of the civil guard resided, and opposite to his quarters were the magazine and armoury. After the convicts were secured for the night the civil guard was marched down in a body from the prison to the barracks, where most of them were quartered, and all rifles and ammunition being deposited in the armoury, the guard were dismissed for the night. This custom was discontinued about thirty years ago.

An excellent library and reading-room, for the use of the prison officers and their families, is maintained by subscriptions, assisted by a contribution from the Directors of Convict Prisons, and in the same building there is also a good billiard-room. Adjoining the barracks is a large recreation-room, and between it and the prison officers' schools is a field set apart for cricket, football, tennis, and other outdoor games. Quite recently the Governor has planted a choice lot of young trees in this field, which will add greatly to the appearance of that part of the village.

Like Chief Warder Hodge, many of the officers spend a much longer time in the prison than any of the convicts ever do. Mr Palmer, the present chief warder, has been connected with the establishment for over thirty years, and Mr Pinch, late principal warder, spent a like term there. The latter who has quite recently left the prison service, and has gone to reside in Plymouth, affords an excellent example of the beneficial effects of the Dartmoor climate, for he looks perfectly fit to do duty for another twenty years. Mr John James, who makes Princetown his home, enjoys two well-earned pensions after his twenty-five years' service at the prison, preceded by a long service in the Royal Marines. He is the possessor of several medals, one being that of the China war.

Perhaps the most most original character ever connected with the prison was Farmer Tom Hannaford, as he was called. He was a native of Dartmoor, and spent his younger days at Lower Town farm, in the parish of Widecombe. For very nearly thirty years he discharged the duties of night watchman without the walls of the prison, often exposed to most inclement weather. He was able to relate many incidents of a more or less exciting character connected with his duties, and as he spoke in the true broad Devonshire, his hearers were both interested and amused. One night on going his rounds he heard a sound which at once caused him to think that something was wrong. It was described by him as 'a zeart ov a scrapy, scrapy noise, like', and in a few moments it ceased. After a short time, during which Farmer Tom remained quite still, he heard the 'scrapy, scrapy noise' again, and then was able to discover whence it proceeded. A convict was endeavouring to escape, and by some means had gained the roof of one of the buildings. Farmer Tom's rifle went to his shoulder

immediately. 'Stap! Stap!' he cried; 'if thee dizzen stap I'll——'
and then he threatened to do something so dreadful that the
convict deemed it the wiser plan to obey the command. After he
retired Tom Hannaford used to give it as his firm conviction that
the prison authorities would never get another man to perform the
duty of night watchman so efficiently as he had done. His widow
now lives at Round Hill Cottage, not far from Two Bridges.

For twenty-three years the Rev Clifford Rickards was chaplain
at Dartmoor Prison. Previous to his coming he had spent eighteen
months at Portland and three years at Fulham in a similar
capacity, so that much of his life was passed in ministering to the
spiritual needs of those who had broken the laws of their country.
Notwithstanding the severity of the winter climate on the moor,
Mr Rickards never missed a morning service, although these are
held at 6.45 a.m., nor was he ever absent without leave. But it
was not so much at the chapel services that good was done, Mr
Rickards thought. It was during his quiet talks with the prisoners
in their cells that he was able to impress them most, and there is
reason for believing that in many instances his work was attended
with happy results. Not a few of his 'parishioners' as he called the
convicts, were really grieved when it became known that he was
about to leave the service, and many put down their names to see
him in order that they might wish him good-bye. Mr Rickards
retired from the prison service early in 1900.

Another officer in whom the prisoners have had a good friend
is Dr Frew, who has been in residence at Dartmoor about twenty
years, and who is now retiring. He came to the prison from
another, and during the whole of the time he has been at Princetown has acted as senior medical officer. He has always been
known as most kind and considerate to those under his care. The
deputy medical officer is Dr Forward.

The prison farm consists of about 2,000 acres, of which nearly
1,500 are under cultivation; the remainder of the ground has not
yet been broken. This includes about 100 acres of trees, many
thousands of which have been planted during the past three or

four years on that part of the farm extending from the Rundle Stone and Two Bridges road towards Mis Tor. The ground having been well drained and prepared for these trees, they are making good progress. Quite close to the prison are large gardens, covering about 50 acres, and these are under the superintendence of Mr Mudge, one of the warders. Here large quantities of vegetables are grown for use in the prison. The Devon cattle on the farm number about 200; there are also about 100 horses and ponies and between 300 and 400 sheep. The farm is under the management of the bailiff, Mr Gourley, who is assisted by a competent staff.

Additions to the buildings, and various improvements, both within the walls of the prison and on the farm, are constantly being made. A large new prison building is now in course of erection, and will probably be completed next year; and in addition to a laundry and a blacksmith's shop, fine stables for the horses working on the farm have just been built. The accommodation is excellent, there being a number of good stalls and roomy boxes, and also a large covered yard, in which horses may be exercised during bad weather. It is of such a size that at the last farm sale the cattle were sold there, and it made a capital auction ring.

On the whole the prison officer speaks well of life at Dartmoor; what the convict thinks of it is quite another thing. 'Crutchy Quin, 10 and ticket' has very kindly left us his opinion on the matter, and has also let us know what he thought of other similar establishments. Not being provided with a notebook and pencil, he inscribed his impressions with a nail on the bottom of a dinner can, where they were discovered by Mr Michael Davitt during his incarceration in the prison.

> Millbank for thick skins and graft at the pump;
> Broadmoor for all lags as go off their chump;
> Brixton's for good toke and cocoa with fat;
> Dartmoor for bad grub, but plenty of chat;
> Portsmouth's a blooming bad place for hard work;
> Chatham on Sunday gives four ounces of pork;
> Portland is worth all the lot for to joke in—
> For fetching a lagging there is no place like Woking.

THE ANTIQUARY

DARTMOOR appeals to all who delight in the study of the past. Those for whom traditional stories, ancient customs, and folklore possess a special interest find it a field in which they may work with a certainty of reward; on its borders the ecclesiastical antiquary meets with much worthy of his notice; while the archaeologist is there able to conduct his researches under conditions which could not be more favourable. There is ample room for all; not a small matter when we remember the speculations in which they are prone to indulge.

It is to its stone remains that Dartmoor chiefly owes its reputation as the happy hunting-ground of those who love things that are old. Vestiges of the dwellings and the sepulchral monuments of an early people are abundant, and of these there are examples of nearly every kind known to the antiquary. It is true the moor can show nothing comparable to Stonehenge or Avebury, or the megalithic monuments that exist in other parts of England, but there are nevertheless some objects that are by no means lacking in importance, while its clusters of ruined dwellings, often surrounded with a massive wall, exhibit some of the finest and most curious hut circles anywhere to be found. And the comparative small size of some of the Dartmoor monuments is in a great measure compensated for by their number. The visitor will meet with nothing that calls forth the wonder with which he regards the trilithons of Stonehenge, but except on the fen, where Nature has forbidden man to settle, he will, as he rambles over the waste, constantly light upon the stones set up in a long past day, often intermingled with blocks of granite that dot the heath, as Mr E. W. Brayley, in Moore's *History of Devonshire*, so justly observes in the same manner as those large fragments which Scott tells us were popularly called the Grey Geese of

Mucklestane Moor. Into the question of the age of these remains and their purpose, or by what people erected, we do not here propose to enter. The intention of the rings known as hut circles is, of course, sufficiently obvious, as also is that of the kistvaen and the cromlech. Various conjectures have been formed with regard to the larger circles and the stone rows, sometimes called by the misleading name of avenues, but these, like the cairns, there can hardly be a doubt were sepulchral in their character. Our present intention is to note what the antiquary has done during recent years, and what he is still doing, and this will also lead us to notice something of what the vandal has done as well.

In the eyes of the Dartmoor man, by which we mean the moor farmer and the labourer, the pursuit of the antiquary is regarded as a craze, and the archaeologist as one almost to be pitied that he has not something better to do than to trouble himself about 'a passel ov ole stones', though a few of the more intelligent view the matter in another light. But I have nevertheless invariably found that they will take some sort of an interest in what you may tell them respecting these remains, and they are always ready to let you know what they have heard concerning them. I know of a case in which some labourers were so desirous of helping the investigators that they actually took the trouble to build a kist they were ordered to search for but could not find. It happened some five or six years ago. A belief was expressed by a couple of antiquaries that a kist would be found in a certain spot, and in their absence the men employed in the work of exploration, having previously inquired as to the kind of object they would be likely to come upon in their digging, constructed a kist of their own, not wishing, so I was informed, 'that the gen'elmen should be disappointed'. They proved themselves to be quite as good kistvaen builders as the men of prehistoric times, for their erection passed muster, one of the antiquaries observing that he was certain such an object would be discovered on the spot he had indicated.

But it is not often that the antiquary is deceived in this way, though instances are not wanting where he has deceived himself. A case which reminds one of 'Bill Stumps, his mark' came to my knowledge some years ago; indeed, it was related to me by the person chiefly concerned, the late Mr C. Spence Bate. He was staying at Merivale Bridge, and one day happened to come upon what he considered to be an ancient monument, and one of a very curious character. It was similar in plan to a dolmen, or cromlech, but its remarkable feature was the capstone, which had been hewn into a circular shape, and its surface smoothed. Instances of dolmens having the rough capstone placed on worked supporters, or pillars, are to be found in India, but a worked capstone resting upon the usual rough supports had not hitherto been observed. Here was an antiquarian discovery of no small importance, and Mr Bate was quite proud of his miniature cromlech. The particulars of the find were communicated to another antiquary—one widely known, not only as having enabled many to derive much pleasure from the study of the past by the light which he has thrown upon it, but also for having initiated a certain movement which has been the means of afford-ing enjoyment to thousands. To Mr Bate's great satisfaction he also was disposed to regard the stone as a true example of a dolmen (though he had not an opportunity of seeing it), and consequently nothing now remained but to write the paper which should record the discovery in the transactions of some antiquarian society. But this was never accomplished. Mr Bate's little son, who had heard all about the wonderful discovery, one day, while his father was in Plymouth, took it into his head to make some antiquarian investigations on his own account. On Mr Bate's return the boy came running towards him with a triumphant look on his face. 'Oh, papa,' he cried, 'I've found out all about that stone for you. I know the name of the man who cut it.' The stone it appeared had been fashioned with the intention of using it for pounding apples, but for some cause it was never removed.

Other stones similar in character to this one, and stones with circular hollows in them, have been looked upon as possessing

H

some claim to antiquity, when they really possess none. At Bulhornstone Cross, near South Brent, a circular stone, about four or five feet in diameter, and having a socket in its centre, was for long believed to be the base of a cross, and its situation at a cross-road lent some colour to the supposition. But many years ago I learnt from an old man that it had been intended for the mill at Owley, and he remembered very well when it was cut. 'Burys' thrown up by warreners have also been mistaken for barrows. I recollect a well-known antiquary once telling me that he had discovered several of these, and imagined them, from their shape, to be Danish barrows. He was about to describe them in a paper, and adduced their existence as a proof that the Northmen had visited Dartmoor, when he learnt that there had formerly been a rabbit warren on the spot, and that his supposed long barrows were only the overgrown shelters of the conies.

The antiquaries of half a century ago were firm believers in the former presence of the Druids on Dartmoor, and when we look upon some wild and solitary scene there it is almost impossible not to regret that their fanciful notions have been exploded. To them the great waste must have been much more than it is to us. Scattered over it they beheld ruined temples, altars, and rock-idols, and on its tors they saw basins hewn out of the granite to contain lustral water and the moving stone of power. They looked upon processional ways over which the white-bearded priests of Odin gravely walked to the columnar circle to perform mystic rites. Everywhere there was that which took them back into a dim past when, as they supposed, things sacred dominated men's minds. Today we, too, look upon the circles and the long rows of stones, but we do not associate the Druid with them. We are not content with imagining that he was once seen on the moor; we ask for proof, and none is forthcoming. The curiously poised logan, and the deep basin on the summit of the tor, we know to be the work of Nature, and not of man. The circle and the cromlech we are unable to connect with any religious idea, and in the stone row we fail to see either a sacred way or a racecourse. We may, perhaps, feel sorry that it is not so, for the stone remains are robbed of much of their interest. In banishing the Druid we have also banished the romance that hung about his supposed temples. But so have we done with regard to the land which as children we were wont to believe was the home of the valiant youth who slew the giant Cormoran, and there is quite as much proof that Jack the Giant-Killer once lived in Cornwall as there is that the Druids were ever to be found on Dartmoor.

It was Polwhele who first brought the Druids to the moor, and every subsequent writer adopted his views. Consequently we find that the Rev E. A. Bray, Mrs Bray, Carrington, the Rev Samuel Rowe, and others, ascribe to them the erection of the menhirs, the stone circles, the cromlechs, and other monuments on Dartmoor; while some have even gone so far as to suggest that they had a hand in piling up the tors. According to several of these writers the early inhabitants of the moor must have passed the greater part of their time in religious worship. Without desiring to reflect upon those who inhabit it at the present day, it cannot but be admitted that there is a great falling off in this direction. Men who now live there find it necessary to give some little attention to the matter of obtaining food and clothing, but their early progenitors, according to the Druidic theory, could have devoted no time to such a trivial purpose. What with dancing attendance upon the Druids when they cut mistletoe in Wistman's Wood, bowing down before Bowerman's Nose, gathering round the Tolmen in the Teign, watching the grand procession at Merivale, the scooping up of water from the Devil's Frying-pan on Mis Tor, or the rocking of the Rugglestone, they could have had no leisure for anything else. And this belief in the Druids obtained even among antiquaries until very recent times. We doubt whether it was quite eradicated until the late Mr R. N. Worth gave it a final blow in 1880 by showing that there was absolutely no evidence that the Druids were ever on Dartmoor, or even in Devon.

Those who have not taken the trouble to acquaint themselves

with modern antiquarian research, no doubt still believe in the former existence of Druids on the moor. The writings of Mrs Bray probably account in great measure for this, and while it cannot be pretended that it is a matter of much importance whether the belief is held or not, it is just as well that the truth should be learned. Those who write or speak on the subject should certainly possess a knowledge of what has been written upon it. Only last week a paper was read at the opening meeting of the Vines Club at Rochester by a former resident of Tavistock, who, according to a newspaper report, dwelt on the evidences which abounded of Dartmoor being a stronghold of ancient Druidical worship. I am not acquainted with the author of the paper, but I venture to express the opinion that he knows very little of Dartmoor literature.

The speculations of the antiquary did not disappear with the Druids. These still continue, and many hasty conclusions have been arrived at. As yet we stand upon ground that is shifting, and know not where tomorrow we may be. Mr Spence Bate was of opinion that the Northmen once occupied the moor, and supposed Grim's Pound to have been erected by an early Viking. The similarity between the interments in the vicinity of that enclosure and those of Norway and Sweden he considered to be strongly in favour of his supposition, and in addition he adduced as evidence a bronze dagger, with gold and amber ornamentation, which he had found near by, as well as place-names existing on the Dart, which he contended had their root in Scandinavian words. But Mr Bate found few followers, and it is doubtful whether anybody now holds similar opinions to his on this point.

The Vikings having gone the way of the Druids, it was necessary to fall back upon the Celts. These served the purpose for a time, and then it was considered that they were altogether too late in the field. Another race must be found that appeared on the scene before they did, and such was accordingly discovered. This necessitated going very far back; but a few thousand years are nothing to the prehistoric archaeologist. It meant a little trouble, too; but that did not signify, for there is no man at once so painstaking and so speculative as the antiquary.

Until the late Mr Francis Brent called the attention of antiquaries to his discovery of stone implements on the moor the existence of these was unknown there. Many specimens were obtained by him, and also by Mr Spence Bate, and the work of collecting has been continued by others, among whom Mr Robert Burnard finds a prominent place. If an antiquary was ever free from speculative theorising it is Mr Burnard, whose work is of the practical kind. The discoveries made by the Dartmoor Exploration Committee of the Devonshire Association have thrown much light upon the early history of the moor. The committee have now made nine annual reports, each one of which has contained something of importance. Flint implements, charcoal, burnt bones, pottery, and other things have been found, and while it is not possible to make Dartmoor reveal the whole of its ancient story, it is, year by year, yielding up portions of it. The spade has done excellent service, but it is to be regretted that its work has been relied upon to too great an extent. Many of the secrets of Dartmoor will never be discovered by the spade. They are locked up in its place-names, and the key to them can only be found in the tongue of the people who bestowed them. Of all the Celtic tongues it is to the Gaelic that we should turn to read that part of Dartmoor history—and it is a large part—on which names are capable of affording information.

Contrasting the present-day knowledge respecting the stone remains on Dartmoor with that possessed by antiquaries only about twenty years ago, it will be seen what great strides have been made. Scarcely any use had been found for the spade; the principal groups of hut circles, and the more notable sepulchral monuments had been examined, and many of them figured and planned, but no turf had been removed. The objects that have helped to give us some sort of insight into the manners of the people who lived in the huts on the moor lay buried in the soil. But these silent witnesses are now coming forward, and much that was once only supposition is with their aid becoming a certainty.

The hand of the vandal is unfortunately only too apparent in many parts of the moor, though during later years it has been in great measure stayed. On the down, on the verge of which I am now writing, there were once numerous cairns; not a single one is now to be seen there, only low circular banks marking their sites. According to a plan drawn in 1832, immediately after a visit to the Drewsteignton cromlech, that monument was then in close proximity to a group of remains finer than anything now existing in the county. Very probably the stones never existed as shown on the plan, but there is other evidence to prove that remains of some kind were to be seen on the spot. Nothing is now to be found there; the spoliator has done his work, and perhaps we ought to feel grateful to him that he did not take away the cromlech as well. Many of the stones have been removed from the rows in the vicinity of Kes Tor; clappers have been intention-ally destroyed; granite crosses have been used for various purposes; ancient enclosing walls have taken the place of quarries, and damage has been done to every kind of object of antiquity found on the moor. It is, however, to be hoped that with the spread of knowledge these things will become more rare, though we can hardly hope for much improvement if there are many on Dart-moor like the farmer whom I heard speaking on this subject the other day. ' I wouldn' tich a stone,' he said—and my heart warmed towards the worthy man on hearing his words, though I speedily found what a mistake I had made in judging him—'I wouldn' tich a stone 'pon the moor that was sticked up—that is, if he was a marked; but if there wudden no letters 'pon un, way I might as well hev'n vur a paus as any other body.'

THE ARTIST

LORD MACAULAY, in noticing the illustrations in Southey's edition of Bunyan's *Pilgrim's Progress*, said that it was with unfeigned diffidence that he pronounced judgement on any question relating to the art of painting. It is just possible that there are those who, possessing even fewer qualifications for such a task, do not share that feeling, and lest I should be reckoned as one, let me at once explain that I have no intention of entering upon it. I merely desire to make a few observations on the work of those brethren of the brush who have sometimes chosen Dartmoor for their subject, or have made it their particular study. I make no pretensions to be an art critic; I only claim, knowing the moor as I do, to be able to tell whether the artist who has painted it has caught its spirit or not. If it were necessary that a man should be a painter in order to know a good picture when he sees it, I should forbear to write another word on the subject, for my own efforts with the brush, as I have already mentioned in this series of articles, have been limited to certain productions of the slap-dash order, a signboard for an inn in the Forest, and a picture executed on the bottom of a table drawer. I congratulate myself now on my choice of a position for the latter.

Northcote declared that Dartmoor was not worth painting. It is only necessary to turn to the works of those artists who have made it their study to understand why this opinion was not shared by others. It is possible to conceive a man, visiting it for the first time and finding himself enveloped in a dense mist during the whole of the day, drenched to the skin and ankle-deep in mire, arriving at such a conclusion, but no one who has seen it under more propitious circumstances would be likely to do so. It would have been much more true had he said that it was not everyone who could paint Dartmoor. Not a long while since an artist who had found work for his brush chiefly under the sunny skies of Italy turned away from the moor with a feeling almost akin to despair.

'I should have to tramp over it for at least six months,' he said, 'before I could venture to begin painting it.' And herein lies much of the secret of success. It takes time to know Dartmoor, and the artist who does not know it, who has not fallen under the spell of this romantic region, who is not fascinated by its rugged hills and its streams all full of life, can never hope to paint a satisfactory picture of it.

It is not to be expected that the artist, any more than he who works with the pen, can give a true portrayal of Dartmoor in all its moods. There are times when Nature refuses to be interpreted. The sunbeam glinting through the bracken, and dancing upon the rippling water hurrying from the turbulent foam that gleams between the moss-coated rocks seeking to check the river's flow, or the pearls that hang upon the grass at early dawn, are not to be faithfully transferred to canvas. But he who has carefully marked the varying effects of cloud and sunshine upon this land of tors and brawling streams, who has caught its colour and its atmosphere, can give us such a picture that when we look upon it we are able to exclaim, 'Here indeed is Dartmoor'.

And in justice to the artist it must be noted that he has to refrain from depicting many of the beautiful effects that he sees, although well able to do so. And this for the reason that his picture would not be regarded as faithfully representing Nature. Who that has wandered on the moor at daybreak in the summer can dispute this? Take your stand upon some rocky height and look down into the deep valley filled with morning mist. How wonderful is the colouring. Its shaded portion is a pure ultramarine, and as it slowly rises in fantastic wreaths and is lighted by the rising sun, the lines are gorgeous. On one side of the valley the tors are 'bathed in floods of living fire'; on the other they are silhouetted against a golden sky and show as one great mass of unbroken purple. To depict this the brightest colours of the palette would be needed—and what would be the effect of these? But it is, nevertheless, a picture that the old moor can show, though no artist would care to reproduce it. Similarly a sunset on the moor is sometimes such that most would shrink from painting, for those who had not seen such a one would doubt the truthfulness of the portrayal. A lady who was looking at one of Turner's pictures ventured to remark to the painter that she had never seen a sunset like the one it represented. 'No, my dear madam,' replied Turner, 'I don't suppose you have. But wouldn't you like to?'

In every part of Dartmoor will the artist find subjects for his pencil, though it is on its verge that the most charming scenes occur. Here in that narrow borderland between the cultivated country and the stony hills, where the streams sweep down to the wooded vales, are picturesque old farmhouses, grey stone bridges often partly covered with ivy, furze brakes through which a path perchance leads to the commons beyond, river banks where slender ash trees bend over the water, and a hundred other objects that form good material. Further away from cultivation are great breadths of moor clothed with heather, and grassy slopes dotted with boulders, often beautifully coloured; streams where cascades are met at every turn; and hills crowned with the grey tor. No matter where he may wander, he who has an eye for the beautiful in Nature will find it on the moor. Even in its recesses, where there is nothing of life, and the new-born streams filter slowly through their boggy channels giving no promise of what they are soon to become, there are spots, like bright oases in the desert, that offer a reward to those who will be at pains to seek them.

John Syer and William Widgery were the first to disprove the statement of Northcote; they were the pioneers of Dartmoor painting. Those who know the moor must admit that their pictures show that they studied it in its varied moods. They may not always be correct representations of places, but the features introduced never fail to be true to Nature. In this connection Mr Widgery was wont to observe, 'I don't want a portrait; I want a picture.' One day, when he was busy painting, a passer-by who had a slight acquaintance with him stopped to look over his shoulder at his work. He could not recognise the view before him as that which the artist was painting. In the foreground instead of a marsh there appeared a rocky stream. 'Mr Widgery', said the visitor mildly, 'there is no river at the foot of that hill.' 'Isn't there?' returned the artist, without looking up; 'well, there ought to be.' Widgery built a house at Lydford, now a private hotel, and thus being close to the moor he was able to study it not only in the golden days of summer, but in its grander aspect under a stormy sky. He died in 1893, and his mantle has fallen upon his son, Mr F. J. Widgery, who paints Dartmoor with excellent effect.

Every artist appears to be more or less of the opinion of William Widgery, that pictures, and not portraits, are wanted. I have never quite been able to understand why. We all know that objects occur in certain views that would utterly spoil a picture if they found a place in it, and no one even with the faintest instincts of the artist would wish to see them there. In such a case it is therefore better that the picture should not be a faithful representation of the scene. But why should it not be so where no such objects occur, and incongruous features are not found in the view? There would be no reason, further than that it might prove misleading, and the artist could very well be allowed to believe that he was able to improve upon Nature. But when it is put forward as delineating some particular spot we do expect that it will bear something more than a general resemblance to it. I have had pictures put before me with the remark, 'Of course you know that', when I have not been able to form the faintest notion what places they were supposed to represent, though explanation proved that I was quite familiar with them. I have no doubt that every painter will consider that I am altogether wrong in my ideas on this matter. The only artist who may possibly agree with me is the one who uses the camera, and even he, it is more than likely, would be only too glad to follow the example of the painter were such possible when a lamp-post or a factory chimney obtrudes itself on the view he wishes to photograph. In this connection the opinion of the Scotch peasant may be recorded. The story goes that one of our leading

'In along' and 'Out auver' The Duchy Hotel, Princetown, before the 1908-9 rebuilding

'In along' and 'Out auver' The arrival of the Prince and Princess of Wales at the Duchy Hotel, Princetown, 10 June 1909, after the rebuilding

The Hotelier Aaron Rowe, of the Duchy Hotel, Princetown, and great friend of William Crossing. No article on the Dartmoor hotelier was written, but Aaron Rowe is mentioned several times in the text and organised the 'testimonial' quoted in the introduction

artists was painting in the Highlands, when a peasant approached, and watched him at his work. 'Mon,' he asked at length, 'do ye never use a camera?' 'No,' was the sharp reply. There was a pause, and then came the remark, 'It's a hantle quicker.' 'I suppose so,' said the artist, working busily. The man began to move off, but not without firing a parting shot: 'An' it's mair like the place!'

Dartmoor is a favourite subject with several present-day artists, who for the most part exhibit a good knowledge of the region. No-one who is not a stranger to it can look upon the pictures of Mr Charles E. Brittan without being conscious that they breathe its spirit. They are distinguished by a charm of colour, while his effects of light and shade on cloud are wonderful. Who that has seen Mr Baragwanath King's border scenes will not admit their fidelity, or that of his pictures of the moor when it wears its summer garb of purple? The cattle and sheep of the hills, and the half-wild ponies which roam over it, have a faithful delineator in Tom Rowden; while W. S. Morrish, a keen observer of Nature, possessing a full knowledge of the country he loves to paint, has given us some splendid pictures of the glorious heather which is its pride.

Probably none of our Dartmoor artists know the moor better than Mr A. B. Collier, who was painting it more than half a century ago, and still continues to do so. And it is certain that no artist is more true to his original. In his pictures the features of the moor are never exaggerated; one does not find the tors made to look like the Grampians. His endeavour is to depict the moor as it is, and in this he is not unsuccessful. Another among our older artists is Mr G. H. Jenkins, whose works show how closely he has studied Dartmoor. The pictures of Mr Arthur Enock, famous for his evening scenes, and Mr J. Barrett are well known, and will always claim attention. While they continue to use the brush our West Country highlands will not want faithful delineators. Mr Eustace A. Tozer makes a special study of sunrise effects and Dartmoor mists, and his work shows much knowledge and observation. His attention has been chiefly devoted to that part of the moor made so famous by William Widgery. His studio is close to the ancient keep of Lydford Castle, and a walk of ten minutes will take him to the commons. Being thus so happily placed Mr Tozer has opportunities for studying Dartmoor at all times and seasons, and that he has made good use of them his works amply testify.

Although the majority of our Dartmoor painters depict the moor in its summer dress, I cannot but think that the late E. M. Wimperis, sometime vice-president of the Royal Institute of Painters in Watercolours, was right when he said that it did not look so well in sunshine as when the mist wreaths hung about its tors. Faithful to his convictions he has given us many fine pictures of the moor when the rain is beating its sides, or when eddying mists half shroud the hills. Dartmoor at such a time looks grand and mysterious, and if its spirit can then be caught the effect is wonderfully striking. But this cannot always be done; the artist perhaps is not on the spot. Naturally he loves the fine weather, and does not turn his attention to Dartmoor when the cloud bursts upon it, and yet Mr Wimperis said that the most valuable notes he had ever taken in his life was when he was wrapped up in a mackintosh; he did not believe, he said, in being a fine weather artist. Whether it is owing to other circumstances, or to the holding of a contrary opinion to that of Mr Wimperis I will not pretend to say, but certain it is that in any exhibition of Dartmoor pictures the studies are, with few exceptions, those of summer effects. Gorse and heather and sunlight we have in profusion, but how few grey pictures. Stormy effects may not be too pleasant a study, but they should not be altogether neglected. The Dartmoor artist is undoubtedly much advantaged by living near to it. Mr Brittan now resides at Dousland; Mr W. S. Morrish, as is well known, lives at Chagford; and Mr Tozer, as already mentioned, finds in the village of Lydford a congenial habitation, notwithstanding that Risdon refers to it as 'a place where no nice nation would have made choice'. But Risdon also speaks of it as being subject to the Dartmoor storms, and this is just what Mr

Tozer wants. When the sort of weather arrives—and he has not often to wait long for it—that would detain most men indoors, he takes a leaf out of the book of Mr Wimperis, and puts on his mackintosh, walks up the banks of the Lyd and takes notes, a 'chiel amang' rocks and dripping fern. It might be imagined that he gets a little damp. Not a bit of it; his clothes do, but nothing can damp the ardour of a lover of Dartmoor.

Painted on the shutters in a room in the Duchy Hotel at Princetown are some exquisite little gems. I have seen it stated that one of them is by Mr B. W. Leader, whose brush has so ably depicted Dartmoor, but Mr Aaron Rowe informs me that he believes it is the work of Mr A. B. Collier, who painted it when staying at the hotel some thirty or forty years ago with Mr Leader.

If there is sometimes a tendency on the part of the Dartmoor artist to exaggerate, it is a fault easily accounted for. The worker with the pen falls under the same reproach, for are not his pictures sometimes overdrawn? Those who are in love with their subjects are naturally prone to magnify their beauties.

Fifty-two years ago a party of six artists, Mr R. P. Collier (afterwards Lord Monkswell), his brother, Mr A. B. Collier, Field Talfourd, Samuel Cook, Philip Mitchell, and A. C. Bell, were gathered in the snug parlour of the Three Crowns at Chagford. The curtain has been drawn upon that memorable evening by the first named, who wrote an account of it in verse in the visitors'-book. This has since been much mutilated, and some of the lines have been lost. I have been favoured with a complete copy by Mr A. B. Collier, from which I extract two verses.

Six artists forlorn, nor shaven nor shorn,
   Of fierce and romantic costume,
Who their moustaches curled at this pitiful world,
   Here indulged their Byronical gloom.

In whisky and water, songs, riot, and laughter,
   These misanthropes took their delight;
And bright flashed the joke through the thick wreathing smoke,
   That vexed the dull nose of the night.

THE VISITOR

HALF a century ago the visitor was almost unknown on Dartmoor, and it was not until many years later that he was to be found there in any numbers, and then only at Princetown, or at Chagford on its borders. A certain few had early discovered its advantages, and sought it during summer, but these were mostly such as lived in the neighbouring parts of Devon, and the tourist, or the visitor from a distance, was hardly ever seen within its confines. To its inaccessibility this was no doubt mainly due; there were no coaches running over the moor, and until some twenty-two years ago Princetown was seven miles from the nearest railway station. When railway communication was opened with that moorland town all this was changed. People who had before only heard of Dartmoor went to see it. Its attractions became known; year by year the knowledge of it spread, until now it is a place much favoured by those who find in a holiday 'far from the madding crowd' greater delight than in one spent in a more populous resort.

That a railway on Dartmoor is an incongruity no one who has a real love for it can deny. The very essence of the moor is its primeval character, and anything that detracts from this is a blemish. But gold weighs much heavier than sentiment. With many the preservation of old-world features is as nought compared with ten per cent. In the present case he to whom the defacing of Nature is abhorrent may not altogether deplore the fact that gold is an unknown quantity, and dividends only visionary. The ordinary tourist probably thinks very little about this. He wants to get to Dartmoor, and is only too pleased that he can do so without any trouble. When there he is delighted at finding himself in such a primitive region, but if it had been difficult for him to reach it in all likelihood he would never have come. From this point of view the Princetown railway is a decided advantage, since it is the means of bringing many acquainted with a most interesting district. Yet we venture to believe that when they begin to learn what the moor really is, a few at least would prefer to have made the journey thither by road rather than that one of its beauties should have been destroyed.

But some of the visitors to Dartmoor never do know what the district actually is. There are those who will not leave the roads; they have heard something of the Dartmoor mists, and do not care to run the risk of being overtaken by one on the open moor. Others have no desire to roam amid the heather; it is troublesome, and their boots are thin. They are willing to believe that there are objects in the wilder parts of the moor that some people consider worth looking at, but the difficulty of reaching them they regard as being so great that they would not think of attempting it. A lady who was staying at Two Bridges last year, and who had been reading Eden Phillpotts' story, *The River*, was so charmed with it that she was desirous above all things, she said, of seeing the spot where its warrener hero had lived in his loneliness. She certainly could not leave Dartmoor without doing so. It was close to Wistman's Wood, was it not; and how far was Wistman's Wood? On being informed she exclaimed, 'Two miles! Oh, dear, I couldn't possibly do that.' And so Nicholas Edgecombe's little dwelling remained unvisited. It is perhaps very enjoyable to wander aimlessly about in the vicinity of one's hotel, or sit on the parapet of a bridge and wait for lunch, but it is not seeing Dartmoor.

Other visitors are very conscientious; they miss nothing that they have settled in their minds is worth going to see. A lady was explaining to her friend how she had seen every part of the moor. 'I don't think we have neglected anything,' she said. 'We have been to a place called Merivale, to look at some stones—they said something about avenues, but I didn't notice those—we saw a lot of tors and several streams, and the prison; we drove to Two Bridges, and Post Bridge, and—let me see—oh, yes, Dartmeet.

I don't think there can be anything more.' Her friend said that was, oh, very nice, but at the same time ventured to suggest that she had not quite 'done' Dartmoor properly. 'No! How is that?' 'Well, you ought to have got in a day or two at Yelverton.'

But there are visitors and visitors, and we are far from saying that all who go to Dartmoor, or even the majority of them, take nothing more than a passing interest in it. Indeed, we maintain that the contrary is the case, and that not a few after a short acquaintance with the district develop quite a fondness for it. This is proved by the fact that the following season sees them there again. The tor and the stream and the lonely valley, possess a wondrous power of fascination, and those who come beneath the spell of the old moor are never tired of seeking it. There are those who have visited Dartmoor regularly for years, and they will tell you that they can imagine nothing more enjoyable than a sojourn among its hills. In my own experience I have never met anybody who said they disliked Dartmoor, though I believe the writer of a certain guide-book was by no means impressed with it. Some may have perhaps felt a little disappointment at first. They have been led to expect mountains, and have found only hills, and these have not appeared to them to be so high as they really are, the cultivated country from which they rise itself being of considerable elevation. But this is forgotten when they get to know the moor, and they soon discover that it is not altogether the height of a hill or the width of a stream that gives them attractiveness. To the Alpine-climber the Dartmoor hills may seem insignificant, yet more than one has confessed to their power. Dwarfed though they may be by comparison with the lofty peaks that are covered with eternal snow, they have not seemed less impressive than formerly to those who have returned to them direct from Switzerland.

Some of the earlier writers on the moor were too prone to exaggerate its natural features and its climatic condition, and this has probably led to much misapprehension. With them the lofty hill was a mountain, and Dartmoor itself very little better than Siberia. We are not going to deny the possibility of finding districts possessing a more genial climate—indeed, we are ready to admit that the task would not be difficult—but we maintain that it is not the land of storms such as it was once pictured any more than it can be called mountainous. But perhaps it is better that I say very little about the latter question, seeing that I have myself been looked upon as one who has helped to disseminate erroneous ideas concerning the Dartmoor hills. To a little book dealing with some of my wanderings on the moor I happened to give the title of *Amid Devonia's Alps*. It was merely, as was remarked by the *Saturday Review*, a poetical title, and was indeed suggested by a passage of Carrington's in which he speaks of 'Devonia's dreary Alps'. But it called forth the ire of a certain gentleman to whom Mont Blanc was not unknown. I was given to understand that such a misleading title would prove fatal to the book, which would have been true enough had everybody felt as he did, for he said that to see a book lying on his library table with such a title as 'Devonia's Alps', while it dealt only with the hills of Dartmoor, 'would give him the jumps'.

To its rugged hills and its clear, rushing streams, Dartmoor owes its wild beauty, and whilst these powerfully impress, especially when seen under certain conditions, it is not entirely to them that the peculiar fascination of the moor is due. That is chiefly born of its solitariness. He who wanders from the beaten track, and passes into its remote places, finds himself in a world totally unlike anything that is seen beyond its rocky barriers. He looks upon a scene that is as it was in the days long before the Roman legions landed on our shores—not a feature has changed. From the busy haunts of men, where the evidences of progress are seen on every side, he suddenly steps into the past. He lives, as it were, in a primeval day : there is nothing to destroy the illusion. It is here that he comes truly under the spell of the moor; henceforth he can never think of its solitary valleys without looking down through the ages.

And it is its solitude that those who would preserve Dartmoor

I

should particularly guard from invasion. While they remain Devon will be able to show that which can be seen in no other part of the kingdom—uncultured Nature without a sign that man has ever intruded upon her domain. The central part of the Forest—the district lying between Princetown and Meripit Hill—has ceased to be as it once was, but the great stretches of moor to the north and to the south are still as ever they were. If these solitudes should be invaded, nowhere in England will the eye be able to look upon a scene in which there is nothing but the handiwork of Nature. No amount of profit, even supposing they could be made to yield such, would compensate for the loss of their primeval character, and it behoves those who believe there is something of more value to a nation than money to aid in the preservation of these stretches of wild moorland, which have come down to us untouched, and in which we have a glimpse of the world as it was.

But Dartmoor is not only a delightful old-world region, where there is much to interest the mind and please the eye; it is also a fountain of health. In this connection its claims have long been insisted upon by the medical profession, no member of which has been so untiring in his efforts to bring before the public what Dartmoor has to offer than Dr W. H. Pearse, the senior physician to the Plymouth Public Dispensary. During a period of twenty-five years he has constantly directed attention to the moor, which as a health resort he declares to be of national importance, and to possess advantages such as are to be found in no other part of our island. Among the valuable papers on this subject contributed by him to medical journals is one 'On Change of Air in Relation to Some Types of Consumption,' which appeared in the *Medical Press* in 1886. In this Dr Pearse points out that 'changes of air,' so small in degree that analysis cannot reach them, have a great effect on the health of the body, and that much benefit is often derived by living for a month, during the summer, an out-of-door life on Dartmoor, even by those who dwell at no very great distance from its borders.

Dr Pearse contends that a much greater benefit accrues from the improvement in health secured to those who seek it on the moor than would result from its cultivation, supposing the latter could be profitably carried out. It is unfortunate that the value of our large open spaces as factors in the preservation of health is too frequently underestimated, although this is becoming more clearly recognised each year. A century ago nobody thought of them but as so much waste land that ought to be enclosed and reclaimed. Those who had an interest in enclosing fostered this idea, with the result that many open spaces were lost to the nation. The poor man saw the common stolen from the goose by greedy landlords, who if they did not, after all, put much money in their pockets, succeeded in doing considerable harm. The journal we have named in referring to the seriousness of the loss should it ever come to pass that the nation be 'deprived of facilities for the physical and intellectual renovation of its people that are afforded to such a valuable extent by Dartmoor', says that 'it is undoubted that many persons are now alive who owe the non-development in them of consumption to the salutary influence exerted on them by occasional excursions to this moor-land paradise; and in the interest of such classes it should be preserved inviolate.'

In *The Journal of State Medicine* for July 1903, Dr Pearse has a paper on 'Phthisis Viewed in Relation to Dartmoor' &c., in which he has given some valuable statistics. Some of the tables show that during a period of ten years, in a number of the Dartmoor parishes, there were no deaths from consumption. Dr Pearse, in concluding a paper which those who have hitherto not sufficiently estimated the value of our Devon uplands as a health-giving district would do well to consult, says, 'It is a well-established fact that the summer months spent on Dartmoor give, in their physical and psychical influences, a renewal of life to the faltering vital energies. This is especially so to those in the hovering failures of vital energy of prephthisis.'

The accommodation for visitors to Dartmoor and its neigh-

1*

bourhood has during late years been greatly improved. Among the proprietors of hotels there is perhaps a lack of knowledge of the district : they are often unable to afford the tourist the information he requires. This is rather unfortunate, as he is not only unable to oblige his visitor, but by confessing his ignorance of what there is to be seen in the locality, and the way to see it, conveys the impression that there is nothing worthy of particular notice. From these remarks we must except our host of the Duchy Hotel at Princetown. Mr Rowe is indigenous to Dartmoor : he is a part of it as much as its heather. Consequently he feels that love for it born of long association, and is never happier than when he can give his visitor information concerning it. Nay, more. He will not only tell them what they want to know about any place in his neighbourhood, but he is always ready to take them to it if they wish.

One suggestion I would make to the hotel-keeper on and around Dartmoor. It is that he should have a 1-inch Ordnance map of the moor hung where all might see it. On this the Forest boundary line should be distinctly marked, and the border common nearest to the hotel coloured with a pale wash. This he would find of very great advantage to him when directing the visitor, and it would also be of much service to the latter.

One more suggestion. Let the railway company run open carriages on the Princetown line during the summer. Visitors would then have an opportunity of viewing scenery such as no other line in the kingdom passes through.

COACHING

LADY HOWARD'S coach of bones in which she used to ride to the moor; a coach and four stated by tradition to have been driven up Diamond Lane, a narrow way leading to the commons in the parish of Brent, and the spectral coach which certain individuals have declared they have seen at dead of night on the moorland roads, are the earliest vehicles connected with Dartmoor of which there is any mention. But these conveyances were of a very shadowy description, their existence resting on no better authority than that of someone who had 'heerd tell' of someone else who once knew a person who said his uncle had seen them; and as we desire something more substantial on which to base our remarks, we will not consider them here. It would not be difficult to show the probable origin of these stories, but they do not belong to present-day Dartmoor, for we are not aware that anyone has professed to have seen either of the coaches for a long time, and they are therefore outside the range of our observations. We are concerned only with those which have a real existence.

Coaching excursions on Dartmoor had their commencement over twenty years ago, when Mr Wolfinden, of Bovey Tracey, instituted a service from that town, and he conducted it for a considerable period. In 1882 Mr John Joll, of the Dolphin Hotel, also started a service at Bovey, and this is still continued by his successors, Messrs Hellier and Lee. In the early days four trips weekly were run, and these became so popular that in 1889 it was found necessary to increase the number to six. The present system of running two trips daily was originated in 1891, and as in 1899 the Newton Abbot Coaching Co also commenced to run over practically the same route as the Bovey coaches, the visitor to the neighbourhood of either of those towns has the choice of several excursions daily over that part of Dartmoor near to which they are situated. In 1887 coach services were commenced at Moretonhampstead and Ashburton, but the latter was discontinued at the close of the 1888 season. The route has, however, recently been again worked by Mr A. W. Cove, of the London Hotel. The Moretonhampstead coach, which is run in connection with the Great Western Railway, was started by Mr Thomas Truscott, of the Tavy Mews, Tavistock, and continued in his hands until the end of the 1892 season. During the present year it has been horsed and run by Mr Brooks, of the White Hart Hotel, in the former town. For many years there have been two coach services at Tavistock, one being run by Mr Thomas Truscott, in connection with the GWR, and the other by Mr John Backwell, in connection with the London and South-Western Railway. In 1901 a daily service of trips from Okehampton was commenced by Mr J. G. Heywood, of the White Hart Hotel, and trips are also run from that town by Mr Powlesland.

There is no more enjoyable way of seeing Dartmoor, that is so much of it as it is possible to see from the roads, than from the top of a coach. We do not pretend to say that any real acquaintance with it can be gained in such a manner; none but the pedestrian can hope for that, for you cannot know Dartmoor in any other way than by climbing its hills and tors, by tracing its streams to their sources, and by passing and repassing through its unfrequented parts. But a very fair idea of it may nevertheless be gained by those who avail themselves of the excursion coaches, and if they cannot by that means learn so much of the moor as he who explores it on foot, they will at least gather some knowledge of it, and in a much easier manner. The coaches belonging to the different services we have named pass over the principal roads on the moor, and as the places from which they start are situated on all sides of it, the visitor may see something of nearly every part, always excepting the central portions of the four quarters of the Forest. It is not possible here to do more than indicate those parts of Dartmoor that are visited by, or may be seen from, the coaches, but this may be sufficient to show that much more of this glorious upland region is revealed to the excursionist who visits it by coach than might be supposed. Bovey Tracey being the town in which this delightful means of seeing the moor originated, we propose in our brief sketch of the moorland districts through which the coaches pass to first notice the one visited from that place.

What we may perhaps be allowed to call the 'country' of the Bovey Tracey and the Newton Abbot coaches extends from New Bridge, near Holne, on the south, to Beetor Cross, three miles from Moretonhampstead, on the north, the West Webburn forming its western boundary. It does not include any portion of the Forest, but the roads crossing it run through some of the most interesting parts of the common lands belonging to the parishes of Widecombe, Manaton, North Bovey, Ilsington, and others. In this extensive tract a number of noted places and objects are found, and most of them the visitor is afforded the opportunity of seeing. Hey Tor, the prominent pile seen from so many points in south Devon, and the fine height of Rippon Tor, are passed; there is a fine view of Hound Tor Combe as the coach sweeps round its head, with the rugged hill of Lustleigh Cleave beyond. On the common, near New House, the enclosures and hut circles on Tor Hill, known as Foale's Arishes, may be seen, and further on Buckland Beacon, from which is a grand view of the valley of the Dart above Holne Chase. The sequestered church of Buckland-in-the-Moor is visited, and a part of the Buckland Woods are passed through as the coach descends to New Bridge. From the road running over the commons from Buckland Beacon to Swallerton Gate, near Hound Tor, there are fine distant views of the moor, many of the more famous hills and tors being visible. The descent of Widecombe Hill is made, and the village and church in which the early Dartmoor farm settlers worshipped is visited. The coach passes into the valley of the West Webburn, within a mile of the Forest boundary, where the road is carried along the western foot of Hameldon. Grim's Pound, the well-known ancient enclosure, is also reached, where the visitor may see some excellent examples of hut circles. The narrow valley of the East Webburn is likewise included in one of the routes, where the grand tors of Chinkwell and Honeybag rise on one side and the huge mass of Hameldon on the other. Manaton and the romantic Becky Falls are visited by these coaches, and anyone who has gone over all the ground that they cover, if he cannot say that he has penetrated into even one of the secrets of the old moor, has certainly made himself acquainted with not a few of its beauties.

The Ashburton coach, which as already stated was put on the road in 1887, ran to Princetown, and that it was taken off in the following year is much to be regretted. But the hilly nature of the roads rendered the working of the coach a very expensive matter, and the GWR, by which most of the excursionists arrived at Ashburton, could not then see their way clear to subsidise the proprietor. The present Ashburton coach does not run so far as Princetown, though it goes over the greater portion of the route to that place. We are well acquainted with every road on Dartmoor, and in the parishes adjoining it, and we do not hesitate to say that there is none more beautiful than that over which the Ashburton coach runs. There is not one without its attractions; each leads the visitor through a succession of fine scenes, but if we were called upon to judge, we should certainly give the palm to that road over which the excursionist from the ancient stannary town, on the river Yeo, is carried to the Forest, and which brings him back over the bridge at the spot where the two branches of the Dart mingle their waters; and over the glorious hill on which is the farm bearing a name which it is not unlikely connects it with a Dartmoor tenant of 560 years ago, for we find that one who held land there in the time of Edward III was named John de Ollesbrom. The Ashburton coach runs by way of Holne Chase Hill, where there is a fine view of the Chase and the Buckland Woods, to the village of Holne, the birthplace of Charles Kingsley. Above the village the road climbs the hill to the moor gate, a magnificent prospect gradually unfolding itself to the visitor as he ascends. But it is when he is within about forty or fifty yards of the gate that the culminating point is reached. Let him pause and look down upon the valley of the Dart, where thick woods clothe the steeps, to give place at last to the heather-covered brow and the crown of grey rocks. Let him pause and look upon huge Hameldon; upon the long vale of Widecombe, and the tors that overhang it; upon the little sanctuary nestling on the hillside; upon the common, bare and steep, and on the crofts that sturdy yeomen long ago snatched from it. Let him pause and look : he will see nothing finer in Devonshire. Through the gate and on to Holne Moor, that stretches away to the Forest. On the right is that lovely gorge of which Eden Phillpotts has given us such a vivid picture, where Sorrow Scobhull gazed into the water and 'read its bubbles into a dead man's name'. Beyond the gorge rise the fine piles of Mil Tor and Sharp Tor, and the lonely farm of Rowbrook is seen on the side of the hill. Further on the Wenna-ford Brook is passed, whose waters will shortly form a lake that shall supply the far-off town. When the valley is left behind and the hill is reached on which stands Combestone Tor, an extended view of the Forest, with old Bellaford rising in the centre, and the Dartmeet valley far down below on the right, is presented. Down the long, steep hill to Saddle Bridge, which, having crossed, we enter the Forest and on to Hexworthy, a moorland hamlet, where men have dwelt for hundreds of years. Thence to the bridge over the Dart, and by the little chapel, and so on to the road that skirts the plantations of Brimpts. Here we are about six miles from Princetown, but instead of proceeding in that direction the coach turns to the right, and descends to Dartmeet. As it slowly climbs the hill on the further side of the stream the visitor again sees the Forest unfolding itself, as he looks back beyond the romantic valley, and when the summit is reached another grand prospect is spread before him, with Sharp Tor rising above the common almost close to the road. On by Ouldsbroom farm to Pound's Gate, and so down the hill to the grassy plateau by New Bridge, where the pixies were once wont to gather. Up the hill to the Holne road again, and once more down to the Dart, and so home. A glorious drive, and one which the visitor will not be likely soon to forget. If it were extended to Princetown its interest would be greatly increased, and it is to be hoped that if it be in the power of the GWR to contribute to such an arrangement, another season may witness a return to the route of 1887. The Ashburton excursion does not appear to be so well known as some of the others. This is unfortunate, as visitors to the country lose in consequence much of what she has to offer in the beautiful and the romantic.

The routes of the Tavistock coaches are over a part of Dartmoor interesting as containing several objects which have received early mention in connection with it, as well as for the grandeur and variety of the scenery. The road enters the moor between the second and third milestone from the town, and runs for some distance under the bold frontier hill from which Cocks Tor rises. Further on it passes below the ridge on which stand Great Staple Tor and Roose Tor, while on the other side is the curiously-shaped mass of Vixen Tor. Crossing the Walkham at Merivale Bridge the road enters Walkhampton Common, with Mis Tor, one of the most magnificent of the Dartmoor tors, rising high on the left. Passing up the hill, with the celebrated group of stone remains on the right, the boundary line of the Forest is reached at the Rundle Stone, an ancient bond mark unfortunately destroyed a few years ago, though the name is still attached to the spot near which it stood. Here an extensive view is suddenly presented to the visitor, who looks across the Forest to the high ridge of Hameldon, and upon a number of fine tors, the crown of Bellaford being conspicuous among them. Sometimes the coach goes direct to Princetown from the Rundle Stone corner, and at others descends the hill and reaches it by way of Two Bridges, very near to which is Crockern Tor, on which the ancient stannary parliaments were formerly held. A halt at host Trinaman's Two Bridges Hotel to enable the passengers to visit some of the places of interest in the immediate vicinity, and then the coach ascends the hill to Princetown, passing the old bridge at the Ockery on the way. A stay in this, the chief moorland settlement, and then a fine run over another part of Walkhampton Common, the Forest being left when the boundary-stone on the outskirts of Princetown is passed. Descending Peak Hill, the coach turns aside to the Burrator Lake, and reaches Dousland by way of Yennadon. From Dousland the route lies over a part of Roborough Down to Horrabridge station, whence a run of four miles finishes a journey full of interest.

Another of the Tavistock routes enables the visitor to see a great deal of the north-western frontier of Dartmoor. It is a very favourite one, as not only is the moor visited, but also the famed Morwell Rocks, on the Tamar. On leaving the old Abbots' House at Morwell, which is near the crags, the coach runs to Chip Shop, and passing near Lamerton, reaches the shoulder of Brent Tor, with the little church on its summit quite close. After a brief halt at the Herring Arms the coach runs to the Manor Hotel, near Lydford station, where there is another halt. In the grounds of the hotel is the celebrated Lydford waterfall, in the midst of scenery of the most romantic character. Soon after passing the Manor Hotel the coach crosses the deep chasm spanned by Lydford Bridge, and climbing the short but steep hill beyond it, enters the village, in which are the remains of the old castle so intimately connected with Dartmoor story. During the whole of the run from Brent Tor the moor has been in full view, but it is not entered upon until Black Down is reached on the homeward journey. From this fine common there is a view of the borders of Dartmoor extending from the Sourton Tors to the Dewer Stone Hill. Tavy Cleave is also partly seen, being marked by the fine pile of Ger Tor, and the cluster of tors that overhang the ravine. A view is also gained of the summit of Fur Tor, the most remote of the Dartmoor rock-piles, which is seen peeping over the ridge on which Lynch Tor stands. On leaving the down the coach passes through Black Down village whence Tavistock is distant four miles.

There is no road running directly on to the moor from Okehampton, but there are two which skirt it for a considerable distance one of them entering upon it, and running along its verge for a few miles. The former is the Tavistock road, and the coach excursion over this one, which extends to Lydford, affords the visitor magnificent views of Dartmoor's loftiest hills. Yes Tor is plainly seen and other well-known heights in its vicinity. Passing over Prewley Moor, which is a part of Dartmoor, the coach runs through the little village of Sourton, above which rise a fine range of crags. Beyond Sourton, Great Links Tor is seen crowning the ridge which rises from the enclosures on the left, and further on is Arms Tor, above the valley of the Lyd, and Bra Tor, on the summit of which stands the cross erected in 1887 by the late William Widgery, the artist. At the Dartmoor Inn the coach turns into the old road to Tavistock and soon reaches Lydford village.

The other moorland coach drive from Okehampton enables the visitor to see the Belstone West Cleave, and the fine, bold hill of Cosdon. The latter rises above the village of Sticklepath, through which the coach passes. The route is then around the base of Cosdon to Payne's Bridge, where the commons are entered, and there is a fine run to Berrydown. From the road the Gorge of Fingle can be seen, and also the more prominent of the rock-piles in the neighbourhood of Bovey Tracey. On the other hand is the moor. At Berrydown there is a halt, and visitors have an opportunity of seeing something of Gidleigh Chase, and the fine circle and other stone remains near Scorhill. Few parts of the moor are of greater interest than that passed through on this route. The starting-place of the old perambulators of the Forest is seen, or at least the hill close to it, and their footsteps may be traced for a considerable distance by those who are acquainted with the locality, and with Dartmoor history.

The Moretonhampstead coach takes the visitor right across the Forest, its eastern boundary passing close to New House, and its western almost touching Princetown. The coach enters upon the common at Moor Gate, four miles from Moreton, a name which merely indicates the former existence of a gate, for none is to be seen there now. As progress towards the Forest is made many fine tors come into view, Kes Tor being particularly prominent. Just after passing the point where the Chagford road joins the high-way, the visitor looks down upon that part of the Forest which

records show to be the locality in which the earliest of farmers
settled. Many of the existing houses are very old, and much that
is primitive still survives among the people. Passing the Warren
House Inn, which, however, is more often known by its former
name of New House, the coach soon after crosses over Meripit
Hill and descends to Post Bridge, a moorland settlement of some
importance. Here is the finest example of a clapper to be seen
on the moor. Between Post Bridge and Two Bridges the road is
of a most interesting character. It passes through the heart of the
moor, and many tors of more than ordinary interest are seen.

It was on this route that the celebrated coach 'The Queen of
the Moor' ran for so many years. The coach was so named by
the driver, William Pomeroy Clarke, one of the best whips in the
county. He was brought up at the feet of George Sparks, who
was long known as a driver far and wide. Clarke still sticks to the
Dartmoor country, being now in the service of Mr Rowe, of the
Duchy Hotel at Princetown. It was George Sparks who caused
the iron spike to be driven into the rock known as the Lovers'
Leap, in Buckland Woods, to mark the spot on which the late
Prince Consort stood. We remember Sparks very well : he was
one of a race now becoming extinct. He died in the summer of
1884, and was buried at St Andrew's church, Ashburton, in
which town he passed the whole of his days. At the funeral his
favourite grey horse was led immediately behind the corpse.
Another old driver is Abraham Callard, of the Seven Stars Hotel,
Totnes, who was never so happy as when seated on the box.

The success of a Dartmoor coaching season, of course, depends
entirely upon the weather. When this is unfavourable much loss is
likely to result, for the expenses of the coaching establishments
are heavy. Messrs Hellier and Lee keep about forty horses during
the season, and the Newton Abbot Co about twenty. Mr T.
Truscott, who also works the Plymouth road, has from seventy
to eighty in his stables, and Mr Backwell from forty to fifty. Mr
J. G. Heywood, who works another route besides his moorland
trip, keeps about twenty-five.

THE GUIDE

EXCEPT in the Chagford district, guides are unknown on Dartmoor. It is, of course, sometimes possible for the visitor to obtain in other places round the moor the services of someone who will conduct him to the more interesting spots in the locality, but he can never depend upon doing so. It is only when he is at Chagford that he can find anyone who holds himself in readiness to accompany him, and there the Perrotts have regularly undertaken that duty for years. It is not often that the visitor to Dartmoor thinks of providing himself with a guide, for he is usually aware that one is not absolutely needed. On the moor no dangerous places are encountered as in a mountainous region. Unless the stranger should be benighted, or a mist envelop him when he is far from a road, he will meet with nothing worse than boggy ground, or an occasional swamp at the head of some stream. But though a guide be not indispensable, those who do not know the moor will find a ramble in company with one much more interesting than if taken without, and will also probably be spared no little fatigue. It is one thing to go floundering mile after mile over the fen, with no idea of the names of the hills and tors surrounding you, and quite another to be taken over the same route with very little trouble to yourself, and not only learn what it is you are looking at, but also much that is interesting concerning those objects. An intelligent guide is valuable to the stranger, and when this comes to be recognised, and there is a demand for him, it is probable that he will be obtainable at all the holiday resorts on the borders of the moor.

Of course, it is quite possible for one who is an entire stranger to the moor to make his way across it, with the aid of a map and compass, to any point he may desire, but nothing is more certain than that he would find himself oftener than was pleasant

142

on boggy and treacherous ground. The stranger marks out a line for himself, and follows it, frequently referring to his map, until he reaches a mire which he finds it impossible to cross. Then he holds a consultation with his companion, but they are undecided whether to go to the right or to the left of it, and they look again at the map. The mire is not shown, so it is folded up and put away. They will soon get to the end of the swamp, they think, if they go a little, say, to the right, and this they therefore do. They have altogether turned from the point towards which they had hitherto been steering; instead of pursuing, we will suppose, a northerly course, they are now going eastward. They hurry forward, anxious to reach the firm ground on the other side of the mire as speedily as possible. Suddenly the foot of one sinks, and pulling himself hastily back, he pauses and looks about him. To their dismay they find that a lateral mire lies in front of them. What had they better do? Shall they retrace their steps, or try to make their way round it? They decide upon the latter, and consequently pass cautiously along its edge. They are now going south, a directly opposite course to the one they had marked out for themselves.

When they reach the end of the smaller mire they find that they are at a considerable distance from the main one, and being determined to avoid it, bear still further to the right. By-and-by they see their way clear to pass it, but when they reach the firm ground beyond they are a good half-mile out of their course. Consequently the map is again pulled out, and the compass consulted. Instead of steering due north, they must now take a north-westerly line, but they have to leave much of it to chance, for they can no longer see the landmarks that were visible an hour ago, as a steep hill confronts them. However, they make their way upward in the direction they judge to be the right one, and on gaining the summit find that the tors present quite a different appearance now from that which they wore when they last saw them, and others have come into view. They are in some doubt as to the wisdom of proceeding, but after another look at the map, continue on their way. In a few minutes they find themselves in the midst of some turf ties. Some are partly filled with water, and finding it impossible to cross them, they have no alternative but to pass along their edges. This necessitates their turning sometimes to the right and sometimes to the left, for the ties appear to be dreadfully mixed up. The ground is very rough, too, and often there are gaps in the narrow strip between two ties that they have to leap across. It is very lonely, for look where they may, only hill and bog are to be seen. 'Nothing that has life is visible,' except some ponies and cattle, grazing on the side of a hill a little greener looking than the rest, a mile or so away. They begin to wish they had not come; but they are half-way towards their destination now, and it will take them no longer to reach it than to return to the place whence they started. Besides, the worst part of their journey may be over. They will go on.

Presently the ground becomes more broken, and progess is difficult. A little further on, and walking is out of the question. The rains have laid the peat bare, and the surface of the hill presents the appearance of a vast sheet of black mud studded with innumerable small islands covered with bog grass. If you look over its surface from a lower level you see only the grass, and no impediment to progress is visible. It is when you attempt to cross it that you become aware of the difficulties. This can only be done by leaping from tuft to tuft, and as it almost invariably happens that after a few minutes of this exercise you reach a part of the sea of soft peat that it is impossible to leap across, and have to return and make a fresh attempt in another place; and as you will probably have to repeat this several times, it will be seen that to cross ground of this nature is a matter to which you must be prepared to devote some little time. So it is with our visitors, who do not succeed in passing over until after many fruitless attempts.

Beyond the fen other impediments are met with. Before they are aware of it they find themselves climbing over the rocks of a clatter, that almost covers the side of the hill, from the summit of which a great tor rises. Further on a flooded stream obstructs their progress, and they are compelled to trace it upward for some distance before they can find a place where they are able to cross. Then the map shows a cart track, or something of the sort, but they cannot find it, which is unfortunate, as it would have led them to their destination. But they plod onward until a glimpse of the in-country is caught, and then the map is again brought forth. Well, they have not done so badly; after all. One of them has left a shoe behind in the bog; the other has succeeded in losing his mackintosh, which fell out of his knapsack when crossing the stream, and also in rubbing the skin off his heels, and they are only three miles from the point which they aimed to reach. Certainly they are dreadfully tired, and their lower limbs are wet, and their stockings stained black by the peat. They have also walked many miles more than they need to have done, but they are nearly at their journey's end now, so it does not matter much. When they return to their homes they will talk of their ramble, and will explain how impossible it is to keep to one's course on Dartmoor, a place where nothing but rocks and bogs and rivers are to be seen.

Now, how different might this ramble have been had someone well acquainted with the moor acted as their guide. There would have been no thought of keeping to any line on the part of their conductor. He would have seen the way as plain before him as the City man does the route from Ludgate Hill to Aldgate. On nearing the first mire he would have kept a little down the valley, and so struck a peat track that passed through one part of it, where the ground was covered with pebbles, and this would have brought him to the little stream that trickled from the morass, and where there was a ford, and a few small stepping-stones. Then he would have followed the track where it passed up the hill to the turf ties; a rough way, certainly, but hard and dry. At the point where the track had its termination he would have struck out towards a narrow gully, through which the winter rains were carried to the valley, and its sides being drained, were firm and covered with turf. This would have been his path, and so he would have avoided the fen which covered so much of the hill. He would reach a part of the valley where were cattle and ponies, showing that the ground was passable, and by keeping low down its side would not even come in sight of the clatter. The stream would be reached at a point where it was almost choked by huge boulders, which could be clambered over with ease, and in less than a quarter of a mile he would have reached a deserted mine and a road. This would not have been left until the end of his journey was in sight.

I have known very many instances similar to this. One writer of a book on the moor, in taking the reader from Erme Head to Fox Tor, makes him ascend a rough, boggy hill, and pass over abominable ground. It was open to him to go which way he chose, but he had no right to take his reader with him, when a good path exists by which he might have gone direct from one place to the other. The path was, of course, unknown to the writer of the book, but it is one which everyone having a real acquaintance with the south quarter of the Forest knows very well indeed. The moormen call it Black Lane. It is used by them in the summer, and by the hunter in the winter.

The next best thing to a guide for the visitor to Dartmoor would be a guide-book that gave directions how to reach any part of the moor, and the various objects of antiquarian interest to be found upon it. But such a book has never yet been written; all the existing Dartmoor guide-books are guides only in name. They are really brief descriptions of the moor, and generally interesting, but are unfortunately full of mistakes. In these hand-books all the well-known objects, that have been described times out of number, and which are easy of access, receive attention; but the hundred and one interesting objects hidden away among the hills and far from the beaten track are never named. The reason is, of course, obvious. The writers of the books do not themselves know where to find them. Grim's Pound, Spinsters' Rock, the remains near Kes Tor and Merivale, the clapper at Post Bridge, Fice's Well, and such like are invariably noticed, but the reader will look in vain for any mention of the fine examples of pounds in the valleys of the Avon, the Yealm, and the Erme; the fine stone rows on Ugborough, Harford, and Stall Moors; the circle on Stall; the kistvaens, menhirs, and rows in the Plym valley; and the smaller clappers, as at Sherrill and Stannon.

That a real guide-book to Dartmoor does not exist is not surprising. An indispensable qualification for the writer of such to possess is, of course, a perfect knowledge of the district; but an acquaintance with Dartmoor history is scarcely less necessary to him. Though his work be nothing more than a guide-book, he would find that, unless he had studied the latter, he would not produce anything satisfactory, and would be likely to make many mistakes, for his notices of places and objects would often oblige him to touch upon historical matters. He would also need to know something of the bibliography of Dartmoor, so that he might not make an unfortunate choice of authorities. Much has been written about the moor that is utterly unreliable, and too much care could not be taken in the selection of the books to be consulted.

A hand-book to Dartmoor would also have to be written on a totally different plan from any other. An ordinary local guide-book has in most cases a town for its centre, and the various routes are sketched from it. But in a Dartmoor guide-book there would be no centre. Instead of working outwards the writer would work inwards, as it were. He would, in fact, have a number of points from which to work, for if the book is to be worth anything at all as a guide it would inform the reader how to reach any given point on the moor from any town or village on its borders. Of what use are directions for reaching Cranmere Pool from Okehampton to a visitor who is staying at Tavistock? Or how is the tourist at Ivybridge to find his way to Dunnabridge Pound if his guide-book only tells him how to get there from Princetown? The arrangement of the book would thus be unlike that of any existing guide; but the man who writes it will have to have given half his lifetime to the study of Dartmoor.

The rambler who is not well acquainted with the moor will find the latest Ordnance map of great service to him. Those who know it well do not, of course, need to carry one, but it is always wise to take a compass. There will then be no chance of wandering in a circle should a sudden mist gather on the moor, and by keeping to one settled course, or as near to it as the nature of the ground will permit, you must in time reach your goal. Anyone whose knowledge of the moor is only slight should, when a mist gathers, and he is unprovided with a compass, keep going downhill. There are not many level spots on Dartmoor, and if he should happen to be on one when first overtaken, he will, if he continue wandering, find that he is descending at last. When he does so, let him not cease to go down, and he will before long be led to a stream. Then, although his troubles may not be over, for the river may be running in a contrary direction to that in which his home lies, he will at all events be certain of reaching a habitation, or road, if he follows it. It is possible to steer by the wind, and I have done so on many occasions, but the practice is not to be relied upon, for in the event of the wind changing the rambler would be thrown quite out of his course.

Dartmoor mists are very confusing even to those who well know the ground, for objects become so distorted that a mound will appear like a lofty hill, and a granite block resemble a building. But to pass over the moor on a dark night is a much more difficult matter than finding your way in a mist. In the latter you can see the ground immediately around you, but in the darkness one is continually stumbling. I am able to keep a fairly straight line in a mist by carefully observing the objects— tufts of grass or heather—a few yards in advance of me, and therefore I never trouble much about them. In the darkness it is not so much a question of keeping a line as of feeling your way, and of the two the latter is much the more difficult.

The late James Perrott was the first regular guide to Dartmoor, and of his four sons, three continue to conduct visitors to that part of it in the vicinity of Chagford, while the fourth will take upon himself the duty if needed. It has happened that all four have been with parties of visitors to Cranmere Pool in one day. That is generally the goal of the explorer from Chagford. Those who are not good walkers may visit many interesting places on the moor in that neighbourhood in carriages. Stanford Perrott has driven a pair of horses as far out as Siddaford Tor. It required care, for there is no road much beyond Fernworthy.

Perhaps the day may come when during the season it will be quite a usual thing to see parties of visitors setting out from the border towns, and from Princetown, mounted on Dartmoor ponies, and accompanied by a guide. Of all the means of getting over the moor there is none better than that offered by the sure-footed little animal who is bred upon it. Motors may be all very well in their way, but they will never find a place on Devon's uplands, and would be nowhere with a Dartmoor pony in a race to Cranmere Pool.

'IN ALONG' AND 'OUT AUVER'

THE cultivated portion of the Dartmoor parishes surrounding the Forest was formerly called the in-ground, as appears from various documents. On the old map of the moor in the Albert Memorial Museum at Exeter, which is apparently of fifteenth century date, that part of the parish of Brent lying off the commons is named Brent Inground; and the term was also used in 1611 by Gregory Newman, the vicar of Walkhampton, who in his answer to a bill filed against him by William Hunt, the rector of Lydford, for tithes of agistment, refers to the parishioners putting their sheep to pasture in their in-grounds as well as on the commons. But now all land off the moor is known to the native as the in-country, though he usually refers to that part of the border parishes to which the term in-ground was once applied as 'in along'. It is one of several convenient terms employed by him to denote locality, the chief among the others being 'out auver', 'out along', which does not mean quite the same thing, 'home by', 'higher zide', and 'lawer zide'. With these he is able to indicate the situation of places and objects, or the spots where cattle may be grazing, and however incomprehensible the directions appear to the uninitiated, they are perfectly clear to those to whom the terms are familiar. But the dweller in the border parishes also understands and uses them, though to him 'in along' and 'out along' have a different signification, while 'out auver' also means something more than it does to the Dartmoor man proper. The latter uses it mostly when referring to the further side of a hill, or range of hills; to the borderer it means not only this, but also the waste that lies beyond. Every part of the moor from which he is separated by the frontier heights is comprehended by the term 'out auver'.

'In along' and 'out auver' have always been closely connected.

150

In the parishes adjacent to the Forest are the vills, the tenants of which—dwellers in their cultivated parts that like a broad belt encircle the waste—have from time immemorial possessed rights of turbary and pasturage over it in the same manner as the holders of the ancient Forest tenements. In this belt, too, were the stannary towns. The parliament of the tinners met in the midst of the waste, but the towns at which the tin was weighed and stamped were 'in along'. The sentences upon those who offended against their laws were delivered on the summit of the lonely tor, but the punishment was inflicted 'in along'. The slayer of the King's deer committed his offence in the Forest or on the commons, but it was 'in along' where the stronghold stood, in the dungeon, or on the gallows belonging to which he suffered for his misdeeds. The names of many persons dwelling in the border villages appear on the Court Rolls of the Forest, often for neglecting to repair the moor-gates, or the ways leading to the commons, so that 'in along' had to bear the expense of that which was of as much advantage to 'out auver' as to itself. The bounds of the commons belonging to the parishes 'in along' are through-out one part of them conterminous with those of the Forest, and though this may not have been conducive to friendly feelings, it must, at all events, have frequently brought the Forest men and the commoners into contact. In many other ways was there a connection between the moor and the farm lands at the foot of its border hills, and thus 'in along' and 'out auver' may be regarded as parts of one whole.

And this connection between the two continues today, though the links that bind them together are not all as of yore. The tinners' parliament has long ceased to meet on Crockern Tor, and tin is no more carried to the stannary towns. The last of the King's deer has been slain, and Lydford Castle has become a ruin, its dungeon choked with rubbish, and the site of its gallows forgotten. But the venville rights of the commoners still exist, though since the Duchy adopted the plan of farming out the quarters of the Forest, they are not now exercised quite in the same manner as formerly. The connection, however, is there, for the venville tenants have an interest in the Forest scarcely less than that of the copyholders themselves, excepting that it is the latter's dwelling place. Each parish, it is true, now looks after its own moor-gates, or it would perhaps be more correct to say that they are supposed to do so, and the man 'out auver' does not trouble himself about them; but the parishes still neighbour the Forest, and their bounds march together. But while most of the old links are broken or have become weakened, many new ones have been formed. Indeed, the links are now ties, so intimately is 'in along' now bound up with 'out auver'.

One of the chief ties connecting the moor with the surrounding villages owes its existence to the industries which have sprung up on it in comparatively recent years. This is, however, one that was first formed in medieval times, for there can be no doubt that the tinners who searched for ore on the waste had their homes for the most part on its skirts. But the tie was broken, and not until the nineteenth century was well advanced did a new one of a similar character take its place. The modern industries of Dartmoor, as we have seen in the course of these articles, give employment to a large number of men. The moor itself would, of course, fail to supply them all, and so those who live round it have found among its hills something for their hands to do. The borderer works side by side with the Dartmoor man; often lives beneath his roof during the week; and thus friendly relations are maintained. Many of the villagers finding that their interests lie upon the moor, that they have to look there for employment, are more inclined towards it than to any place in the in-country. They do not, of course, become attached to it in the same way as a native does. His love for it is born with him, and it is but very rarely that he loses it. As a rule he has no wish to leave it, but the borderer would do so without much regret if he found it to his advantage. But until he does he is content to live near its rugged hills; to feel that he belongs to it, as it were; that he is a Dartmoor man, the only difference between him and his brothers of the Forest being that he is 'in along' and they are 'out auver'.

And the borderer takes an interest in much that pertains to the Forest that is unconnected with the industries that have been established there. For many years the Brent Tor & Lydford Pony Society have done good work in promoting the useful breeding of Dartmoor ponies, and have held annual exhibitions. More recently a similar society was formed at South Brent, and in the early part of the present year the Chagford, Gidleigh, South Tawton, & Belstone Dartmoor Pony Breeders' Association was also formed. These hardy animals roam at will over the Forest, and the belief that is entertained in their capabilities, which the movements that have been initiated fully prove, plainly indicate that 'in along' does not lack appreciation of that which 'out auver' produces. And as 'in along' takes an interest in much that is done 'out auver', so the latter does not disregard what is going forward in the borderland. Thus when the Moreton Horticultural Society holds an exhibition, or there happens to be a flower show at Lustleigh, or attractions of a similar kind elsewhere on the verge of the commons, there will generally be found a sprinkling of Dartmoor people amongst those present. But we are hardly prepared to say when there is a concert at Huccaby or at Wide-combe, that many of the border villagers find their way there. Perhaps they would consider those places a little too far 'out auver'.

Among those whose duties frequently take them from 'in along' 'out auver', Mr J. D. Prickman, of Okehampton, is certainly as well-known as any. As Coroner for the district in which Dartmoor is situated it becomes necessary for him to visit Princetown and other parts of the Forest. In former days the duty of holding inquests upon persons who met their death on the moor devolved upon the Coroner of Lydford, as is shown by a document of sixteenth century date, in which it is set forth that 'yf a man dye by mysfortune, or be slayne wtin the said Forrest, mores, and waste, the Crowner of Lydeforde shall crowne and sytte vpon hym, for the said Forrest, mores, and wast is owte of every Tithing.'

Another who dwells 'in along', but is often seen 'out auver', is Mr Thomas Rice, of Lydford. Mr Rice acts as assistant-overseer and collector for the parish, and as this includes the whole of the Forest it is hardly necessary to say that the position is unique. He commenced his duties at Lady Day 1880, and has ever since regularly visited all the houses of the ratepayers in the Forest, with the exception of two or three. These latter comprise Huntingdon warren, at the extreme southern end of the Forest, to which Mr Rice does not go; and East Ockment farm at its northern extremity, and Fernworthy on its eastern side, at which he calls only occasionally. In these cases he either meets the occupiers, or the rates are sent to him. A half-yearly rate is made, but Mr Rice goes over the parish quarterly. It takes five days to collect from the houses in the Forest. A commencement is made at Rundle Stone, and the first day finishes at Post Bridge. The next morning, after the houses in that place have been visited, Mr Rice makes his way to the Warren House Inn, and then collects from the farms in the valleys of the Walla Brook and East Dart, reaching Hexworthy, by way of Dartmeet, in the evening. The third day the farms in the valleys of the Swincombe and the West Dart are visited. Princetown and the few scattered farms between that place and White Works take two days more. Another day is required for collecting in that part of the parish situated 'in along', so that exactly a week is necessary to go over the whole of the ground. It is safe to say that no other rate collector in England has so large a district, and his experiences of wind and weather are such that the large majority of them know nothing of. It is, however, also true that what is to them a common occurrence Mr Rice finds to be a rare one. He is never asked to 'call again'. So he generally contrives to bring 'in along' what he goes 'out auver' to fetch.

Perhaps no man who lives 'in along' goes 'out auver' so frequently as Mr W. Rich of Lake, a hamlet near the little border village of Sourton. Mr Rich acts as caretaker at the peat works at Rattle Brook Head, and he has been connected with them for twenty-four years. During that period there has only been one week that has not seen him at his post, and then illness was the cause of his absence. This speaks volumes not only as to his fitness for the duties which he has been appointed to fulfil, but also as to the healthful properties of the Dartmoor air. Mr Rich visits the works, which are situated just within the bounds of the Forest, and in a wild part, every day. When the works were started, about 1879, a railway was constructed from them to Bridestowe station, for the purpose of sending down the peat, but owing to the ill-success of the undertaking it has never been much used. It does not, however, form the way by which Mr Rich reaches the works, though he, nevertheless, often goes over it to inspect its condition. From Lake he breasts the steep hill rising to the great pile of Links Tor, and does not take the railway for his path until he is near the source of the Lyd, when he is at no great distance from the works. Mr Rich holds fast to the opinion that something will yet be done at Rattle Brook Head. He believes that a way will yet be found to transform the Dartmoor peat into a profitable fuel, and though he has seen more than one attempt made to do so since the original company was formed, and seen them fail, he is not disheartened. Meanwhile he is 'in along' every night, and 'out auver' every day.

A post which has nothing to do with 'in along', but which from early times has been connected with 'out auver', is that of Forest reeve. Anciently the duties attached to the position were very important, but they have now become much less so. The present reeve is Mr William White, of Meripit, but his deputy, Mr Richard Coaker, of Runnage, always acts. There are duties in connection with the drifts that have to be performed, and any dispute that may arise as to the right of common also demands the attention of the reeve, or his deputy. They are elected by the Duchy officers and the copyholders of the Forest, at the Duchy Court held annually at Princetown, at the end of October, or during the first few days of November. At these courts, which are presided over by the deputy-steward, the Forest tenants pay their rent, and all other business connected with the Forest is transacted. No one but those who are actually concerned in this are allowed to be present.

Whether success is more likely to attend the efforts of those whose farm lands lie 'in along' than it is those of the men who seek to make the soil 'out auver' yield them a reward for their industry, is a question the answer to which depends entirely upon the locality that has been chosen as the scene of labour. Speaking generally, there is, of course, no comparison between in-country land and land that has been reclaimed on Dartmoor, but there are nevertheless certain spots on its borders where it is of less value than some that is to be found within the Forest. But the moor is not a spot to which a man must go who wants to grow rich. 'A comfortable living may be made by the small farmer,' a Dartmoor native once said to me; 'that is, you know, if he can put up with a lot, but he'll never make no money.'

Present-day life at Princetown has not very much of the Dartmoor character about it. Though 'out auver' it is so closely linked by the railway not only with 'in along', as meaning the border land, but with the towns scattered down the in-country, that it has much in common with them. Consequently one is not surprised to find that public dinners are by no means functions unknown; that football, cricket, and lawn tennis may be indulged in, or a game at billiards; or that concerts and entertainments help to pass the winter evenings. Princetown is, as it were, a bit of 'in along' dropped 'out auver'.

And now with Risdon I must confess that I have detained you 'on a place so wild, with so slender repast, where it is to be doubted you have taken the cold, or the cold hath caught you; wherefore we will onwards on our journey.' In other words we will turn our steps 'in along', though it may be not altogether without some recollections of 'out auver', and of the life led by the people who dwell there.

INDEX